Kevin Durant: The Inspiring Story of One of Basketball's Greatest Small Forwards

An Unauthorized Biography

By: Clayton Geoffreys

Table of Contents

Foreword

Few players have the ability to score from anywhere on the basketball court. Kevin Durant is one of those players. Since emerging in the league, Kevin Durant has become a superstar in the NBA, soaring to new heights year after year in leading the Oklahoma City Thunder into deep playoff runs. Durant's ability to penetrate to the hoop while also shooting from anywhere on the court makes him one of the deadliest scorers in the game. Playing alongside Russell Westbrook, Durant and the Thunder were a team to be reckoned with every year. After nine years with the Thunder, Durant decided to sign with the Golden State Warriors in the 2016 offseason, joining Stephen Curry, Klay Thompson, and Draymond Green in creating what many consider a super team. Time will tell what this assemble will be able to accomplish together. But Kevin was not always one of the greatest basketball players in the world; his story began from very humble roots, which you will learn about in this book. Thank you for downloading *Kevin Durant: The Inspiring Story of One of Basketball's Greatest Small Forwards.* In this unauthorized biography, we will learn Kevin Durant's incredible life story and impact on the game of basketball. Hope you enjoy and if you do, please do not forget to leave a review! Also, check out my website at claytongeoffreys.com to join my exclusive list where I let you know about my latest books and give you goodies!

Cheers,

Clayton Geoffreys

Visit me at www.claytongeoffreys.com

Introduction

The game of basketball has many facets a player can excel at. There have been excellent rebounders such as Wilt Chamberlain, Moses Malone, and Dennis Rodman, among others. The NBA has also seen its share of passing wizards in the form of Magic Johnson, John Stockton, Jason Kidd, and Steve Nash. And when all else failed, some defenders stopped at nothing to deprive opposing teams of baskets. Names such as Bill Russell, Joe Dumars, Dikembe Mutombo, and Gary Payton excelled at that aspect of the game. But no matter how many ways a player can affect a game of basketball, scoring was always the name of the game. No other player could do that better than Kevin Durant.

Standing over 6'10" and with arms as long as a mile, Kevin Durant had the height and length that was supposed to score baskets inside the paint. However, Durant was also blessed with the athleticism, grace, footwork, and handles that made him an even greater threat with the ball in his hands out on the perimeter. He has the size of a center, but could move like a shooting guard on the floor.

And with the addition of his ability to hit unguardable jump shots and his stone-cold mentality of hitting bucket after bucket, Kevin Durant was a born prodigy at putting the ball through the hoop. And, in that aspect, he was also very efficient as his shooting percentages would show. He has become one of the few members to average 50% from the floor, 40% from the three-point line, and 90% from the free throw line all in the same season.

His natural ability at making buckets has earned Kevin Durant four scoring titles in his ongoing 10-year NBA career. And for the ten years he has been in the NBA, Durant was always one of the most sought-after stars and was the main reason why the Oklahoma City Thunder, his first organization in the league, was transformed into a powerhouse Western Conference team that always had a chance to make the Finals every year.

As Kevin Durant rose through the ranks of the NBA's best small forwards, the Oklahoma City Thunder were also rising as one of the best young teams in the NBA. In his stint with the Thunder, Durant had a successful partnership with Russell Westbrook, who helped him form the league's deadliest duo since Kobe Bryant and Shaquille O'Neal played together in Los Angeles. For all of his dominance as an individual scoring threat, Durant was equally as dangerous when playing with other star talents on the floor.

While Kevin Durant was mostly known for his ability to make scoring look easy, he was not a one-trick pony that relied merely on putting points up on the board. In his 10-year NBA career, Durant also developed into a feared all-around player. With his athleticism and length, KD was one of the best small forwards at rebounding the basketball. With the ball in his hands, he could also create shots for teammates and looked like a point guard on the floor. His defense, which used to be his weakness, also became an impressive part of his game. He could lock down on any perimeter player while also blocking shots inside the paint.

With a transcendent ability to score and mature all-around skills, Durant has become a seven-time All-Star, a six-time All-NBA Team member, a four-time scoring champion, a Rookie of the Year, and an NBA MVP. On top of being considered the best and most complete scorer of his era, Durant is also widely regarded as one of the greatest of his generation and contends with LeBron James and Stephen Curry among others for the crown of the best player of this era of basketball.

Despite being one of the most unique talents the league has ever seen, and despite the fact that he spent the first nine years of his career playing for a team that contended for the NBA title, Kevin Durant is yet to win an NBA championship. He had his best chance in 2012 when his young team lost to the Miami Heat of his rival LeBron James in the Finals. And in 2016, he seemed like he was on the verge of making it back to the Finals to finally win it all before his team squandered away a 3-1 series lead to the Golden State Warriors in the Western Conference Finals.

With that tough playoff loss to the Warriors behind him, Durant went into the offseason of 2016 as one of the hottest free agents in recent years. Wanting to do away with the stigma of being ring-less, Kevin Durant chose to sign with the Golden State Warriors to form a powerhouse combination of an already super team that went 73-9 during the 2015-16 regular season. Joining the likes of All-Star talents Stephen Curry, Klay Thompson, and Draymond Green, Kevin Durant figured himself at the best possible position to win his first NBA title as the 2016-17 season unfolds.

Chapter 1: Childhood and Early Life

Kevin Wayne Durant was born on September 29, 1988, to Wayne and Wanda Pratt in Seat Pleasant, an incorporated city in Prince George's County, Maryland, which is just outside the nation's capital, Washington DC. Both of Kevin Durant's parents were government employees. His mother worked for the US Postal Service while his father was a US Capitol Officer at the Library of Congress.

Wanda was only 18 when she had her first son, Anthony, out of wedlock. Three years later, she gave birth to Kevin Wayne before she married Wayne. This is the reason why Kevin uses his mother's maiden name as his family name. Unfortunately, Wayne and Wanda were not ready for married life. At about the time Kevin Wayne was to celebrate his first birthday, Wayne left and abandoned Wanda and the two kids. He would later go on to say that he did so because he was immature, selfish, and that he did not know what he was getting into.

Left alone to raise her two children and struggling to make ends meet, Wanda and the boys moved from one apartment to another in Prince George's County-Capitol Heights, Suitland, and Seat Pleasant. Life was so tough on Wanda and the kids during those days that Kevin still vividly remembers the first apartment they moved to, which had no bed and no furniture. They just sat in the living room and hugged each other. Despite the hardships, Wanda was determined to give her children a better future.

Wanda continued to work at the Suitland, Maryland Post Office, lifting 70-pound mailbags and loading them onto a tractor-trailer. She worked the overnight shift taking care of the mail, so someone had to take care of little Kevin. That task went to Wanda's mother, Barbara Davis, who lived in a house with her sister, Pearl. Barbara would take Kevin to school, but when she had other errands to do, it was his aunt Pearl that made him jelly sandwiches after school and watched cartoons with him. So, as early as five years old, Kevin Durant learned about the value of sticking together as a family.

Even as a kid, Kevin was already laid-back. His grandmother would pick him up at school, and she remembers asking him at times if he wanted to talk to grandma. Kevin would speak for a minute and then would retire to himself and be quiet. Barbara had no problems raising young Kevin. She said that when Kevin came to their house, he had no problem entertaining himself because he would play alone. He would run to the same spot, plop on the floor, and just disappear. Young Kevin preferred to play on his own because he was shy.

His grandmother also recalled the now-famous "clothespin" story. Kevin would just need a penny and a clothespin, and that was it. He played with both for hours and hours, sitting on the floor with a penny and a clothespin. According to Wanda, this went on for years until she finally asked her young boy what he was doing. Young Kevin answered that he was making up basketball plays.

Basketball finally entered Kevin's life when Wanda was driving eight-year-old Kevin to get a haircut. Along the way, they passed by Saint Pleasant Recreational Center, and Wanda thought that the Center would be a good place to leave both Tony and Kevin on Saturdays because she did not want them to depend so much on Barbara and Pearl. She registered them there, and the following week, she told Tony and Kevin that they were going to the gym. Little did Wanda know that their lives would soon change because of that gym.

Kevin remembers the first time he opened the gym doors, and all he saw were kids and coaches. He said it looked like an amusement park, and he immediately felt at home because it seemed to him that the children were waiting for him, much like how his Aunt Pearl waited for him at his grandma's house. Durant had played only occasional basketball back then. His basketball world was more of the "penny and clothespin."

However, once he started dribbling the ball and shooting hoops, he lost his shyness.

When a coach whom the kids fondly called Chucky approached him and asked if he wanted to try out for the Center's 9-and-under basketball team, Kevin confidently replied, "Why not?" Hence, the story of Kevin Durant and his early mentor, Charles "Chucky" Craig, began. Chucky taught Kevin the basics of the game. When the tryouts were over, the name "K. Durant" was included in the final roster for the Center's 9-and-under team. Charles Craig gave Kevin Durant the jersey number 24.

Kevin went home and showed off his jersey number to Wanda, Barbara, and Aunt Pearl. A couple of weeks later, he would score 25 points in a game, which was unheard of for such young children. An unknown woman approached him and told him to change his number from 24 to 23 because he played like Jordan. Flattered, Kevin replied that he wanted to play in the NBA someday and that he wanted a career in playing basketball. When he told his mother of his dream, she said that he would have to put in the hard work, the way she did daily at the Post Office. Kevin took his mother's word to heart, and by the sixth grade, he would take the bus to his grandmother's house and then run 20 minutes all the way to the Recreational Center.

Kevin Durant was starting to become a star prep player as the years went by. It was when he was about 11 years old that Kevin finally noticed that Aunt Pearl never came to see him play. He was unaware that she had breast cancer. One night while the whole family was at his grandmother's house, Pearl started to spit blood. Sadly, she had already passed before the paramedics arrived. As the paramedics cleaned her up in bed and waited for the coroner to arrive, Kevin lay beside her, mourning the first loss of a loved one that was so close to him.

With Aunt Pearl gone, Grandma Barbara advancing in age, and Mother still working long hours at the Post Office, sixth grader Kevin needed a father figure to lean on. However, his father was busy working as a police officer doing shifts at the Washington Hospital Center in DC. Thus, the logical choice was for Kevin to spend more hours at the Recreational Center with Coach Chucky and another coach named Taras Brown, whom Durant would later call "Godfather."

Brown was an AAU coach who nurtured what Chucky Craig taught Kevin. He noticed that Kevin was somewhat passive on offense, and would not ask for the ball despite having a feathery outside touch. When they talked about going to the NBA, Brown told Kevin that if he did not play like Tracy McGrady every night, he had to run 100 laps. Durant knew who McGrady was and had watched him play, but he did not want to hoard the ball the way T-Mac did because he was afraid his teammates would get angry. Brown and Chucky took Kevin to watch NBA games to drive home the point. Kevin loved the way Celtics' forward Antoine Walker would shake his body after hitting "threes," and that is where his shaking before free throws came from. Durant also envied T-Mac's step-back "three," so he practiced that move, too. Soon, Durant was very close to his coaches and would even sleep on their couches at night after watching pro games.

The Recreational Center would become Kevin Durant's refuge because he started to become self-conscious. One of the reasons why Kevin felt that was the fact that he was always the tallest kid wherever he went. In class, his mom would ask his teachers to put him at the end of lines so that his height would not be noticed and he would not stand out that much. Barbara would console Kevin's insecurity with his height by telling him that his height was a blessing.

Still, it was not only his height that bothered him. In eighth grade, Kevin Durant was just 6'2'', his feet were size 11, and the only shoes his mother could afford were used Lisa Leslie or Cheryl Miller shoes, which she bought from an Eastbay catalog. Despite being a budding basketball star, Durant would walk with his head down in hallways, self-conscious from head to toe. He hated school so much, and the gym was his only haven, which was the reason why he became a better ball player.

Aside from Durant, the Jaguars also featured Michael Beasley, who would later become the number 2 pick of the 2008 draft. PK Martin, the man who ran the organization at the Recreation Center, asked Young Michael Beasley to try out for the Jaguars. When he first played with the kids in the gym, Beasley looked clumsy and awful, even though they all knew he was good. Since he was left handed, Beasley was awkward and at times looked like he was lazy. So after a few hours of practice, he was told to leave the gym. Before he left, Beasley stole the box of pizza the team had ordered for lunch. Beasley later went on to say that he did it because they were so poor that he did not know when he would eat next. That was how Kevin Durant met Michael Beasley, and that is how Beasley first came to the Jaguars.

PK Martin later changed his mind and invited Beasley to come back. From then on, he became a part of the team. Although he would not play much in his early days as a Jaguar, Kevin Durant said Beasley showed his true worth when he scored 20 points and 20 rebounds in a triple-overtime championship game.

As Michael Beasley achieved basketball success, he grew closer to Kevin Durant.

Beasley's mom was a single parent raising four teenagers. She would drop Michael at Durant's place at 6:30 in the morning for breakfast. Newfound best buddies Kevin Durant and Michael Beasley would then ride the same bus to school and play in the same basketball game in the evening.

With Durant and Beasley leading the team, Brown's Jaguars reached near mythical status by winning various national basketball youth championships and beating countless AAU teams in different tours across the country. With the Jaguars reputation growing, so did Durant's.

Durant played with the Jaguars until he was 14 years old. By then, he was old enough to play for the DC Blue Devils, an AAU team loaded with talent and which participated in tournaments with older age brackets because they often wiped away competitions in their division. Rob Jackson, an AAU veteran who was then coach of the Blue Devils, said he took in Durant on a recommendation from Taras Brown. Jackson stated that Durant was not on anyone's radar at that time and that he was not the best player out there.

Durant went on to play as a reserve of the Blue Devils' Team B, initially. It was also known as its "feeder team" because it fed players belonging to their A Team, which traveled around the country from April to September to compete in tournaments that exposed the players to collegiate coaches and scouts.

Chapter 2: High School Years

Kevin Durant spent his first two high school seasons at the National Christian Academy, a privately owned school in nearby Fort Washington, Maryland. The head coach of the school, Trevor Brown, had previously seen Durant, Beasley, and another high school prospect, Chris Braswell, play for the Jaguars. He was amazed at how the three eighth graders played like pros.

Durant spent the first half of his freshman season playing for the junior varsity squad. There, he was a hit as the talented freshman that played all five positions on the court. His success with the junior varsity team made Coach Brown promote him to the varsity squad, which made him only the third freshman in Brown's coaching career at National Christian Academy to play for the school's varsity squad.

When Durant returned to the Blue Devils after his freshman year in high school, he had grown from 6'3" to 6'7" and had become a two guard and swingman in a big man's body. Blue Devils' Coach Jackson knew that Durant was ready to make an impact. He promoted Kevin Durant to the travel team where Durant teamed up with future University of North Carolina and Denver Nuggets point guard Ty Lawson in the backcourt.

Durant reminded Coach Jackson of Houston Rockets' Tracy McGrady and Dallas Mavericks' German import Dirk Nowitzki, who were both big men able to score inside and outside. Brown took notice of how Durant caught a pass, took the shot with proper form, and released the ball with perfect rotation. However, what made Durant unique was that he had something more that many kids did not have -- desire. Jackson said he had never seen the kind of passion Durant had. The kid was ultra-talented, but he still wanted to be better each day.

At National Christian Academy, Coach Brown also attested to Durant's work ethic. Brown said he had never seen any kid devote himself that much to basketball. After Durant practiced on the maroon rubber court of National Christian, he would take a ride to the Saint Pleasant Recreation Center to practice some more. Durant was driven, and he had no other desire except basketball because the people around him were basketball people. His coaches were like parents to him. They were his biggest supporters, yet when he was wrong, they were also his biggest critics. His mother wanted it that way. She knew early on that Kevin responded well to the reinforcement he had at home.

Durant led National Christian Academy in scoring as a sophomore. He played center on defense because he was the tallest player on the team, but switched to two guard or small forward on offense because he was the team's best shooter and scorer.

Crowds of over 500 people came to watch Durant play at National Christian's small gym. At some games, people had to stand on the stage to watch the sophomore sensation strut his wares. The Eagles posted a 27-3 record that year, the best in the school's history. Everyone started to take notice of Durant, and Coach Brown's mailbox began to fill up with solicitations from collegiate coaches.

In November of that year, the Eagles played in an annual tournament called War on the Shore in Milford, Delaware. Dozens of college coaches attend the tournament to get a first look at the new crop of underclassmen that were playing to earn a collegiate varsity slot.

University of Texas assistant coach Russell Springman was at the tournament to scout someone else. However, it was the lanky sophomore from National Christian Academy that became the apple of his eye. Springman had an eye for big shooting guards and tall small forwards. He liked to recruit what he called "hybrid kids" who would revolutionize the basketball positions as we know them.

Springman said he never saw the entire game that National Christian played. All he needed to see was Durant launch and nail a three-pointer from the corner, and that was it. He became intrigued with the kid who played guard on one end and center on the other. Springman pulled out a player profile, a paper that launches the recruiting journey of an underclassman, and wrote Kevin Durant's name on it. Shortly after the tournament, Springman made Texas the first college to officially express interest in a future star by calling National Christian Academy Coach Brown and inquiring about Durant.

Before his junior year, Kevin Durant and Blue Devils Head Coach, Rob Jackson, visited Oak Hill Academy, which was 360 miles from Maryland. Oak Hill was a 129-year-old Baptist School with around one hundred and fifty students from grades 8 to 12. They also had the most dominant prep basketball program in the nation. Former NBA star, Ron Mercer, once scored 41 points for Oak Hill, while another former NBA star, Jerry Stackhouse, was the 1993 Nike MVP there. Knicks Superstar Carmelo Anthony played at Oak Hill before going to Syracuse, and future Atlanta Hawks superstar Josh Smith is Oak Hills' top single-season scorer.

Oak Hill coach Stephen Smith met Durant, Jackson, and another prep star, Ty Lawson, who went with them on the trip. Smith immediately got the two kids ready for a workout. He let Kevin Durant defend Josh Smith. To his surprise, Durant, only 15 years old at the time, played it even with Josh Smith, who would forego college later that year to become the Atlanta Hawks' first-round pick. It was touch-and-go from there.

When Kevin's mother heard about them going to Oak Hill, she immediately approved of it because she said that every other kid wanted to go to Oak Hill. She thought it would be big, and it was.

Durant joined the Oak Hill Warriors together with longtime friend and teammate Ty Lawson. Kevin Durant would start every game with the team. With Oak Hill having future Syracuse starter David Devendorf, and Jamont Gordon of Mississippi State at its backcourt, Durant was shifted to power forward where he trailed on fast breaks and caught his passes at the three-point line where he could shoot or take the ball to the basket. Again, Coach Smith noticed a long-time "defect" in Kevin Durant's game -- he did not demand the ball.

Smith said he looked passive at times, and although he was not a liability on the court, Coach Smith noticed that there were moments when Kevin Durant could have just taken over the game by himself. Instead, he let his teammates join the fray.

However, there was a game in Portland where Durant would mark his legacy at Oak Hill.

The Warriors were playing in a semifinal game of an invitational tournament in Portland. With the Warriors down late in the fourth quarter to a nationally-ranked team, Coach Smith called a timeout and called for a rare five-out motion set offense, which required all of the players to drive to the basket.

Unbelievably, Durant would then hit a three-pointer, complete an and-one play, and hit another "three." Less than forty seconds later, the game was tied. Then Durant continued to score. He scored all of his 13 points in the closing moments of the match, which they would win in a thrilling come from behind fashion.

Oak Hill would go 34-2 that year, and Durant averaged 19.8 points and 8.8 rebounds to lead the team. Durant's ascent to national basketball began and he had one year left before college. For his senior year, Durant transferred to Montrose Christian where he would average 23.6 points, 10.2 rebounds, 3.0 assists, 3.0 steals, and 2.6 blocks per game. He would be named First Team All-American by USA Today and co-MVP of the McDonald's All-American game after scoring 25 points for the West Team. Montrose Christian went 20-2 that year to finish with a ninth-place ranking in the nation.

Chapter 3: College Years at the University of Texas

After the conclusion of the 2005-06 season, Kevin Durant took his official recruitment visit to the University of Texas, remembering that it was the first school that took notice of him when he was still a high school sophomore. Durant and his mother were impressed with the persistence of Assistant Coach Russell Springman, who previously scouted Kevin Durant at the War on the Shore tournament two seasons before. When Durant's father Wayne called up Springman to arrange their Texas visit, they were told that Longhorns' Coach Rick Barnes let his players do what they did best. He also assured Pratt that they would take good care of Kevin.

Hence, for a family with close ties, the Durant's had zeroed in on the University of Texas before any other college. When Durant and his father made their first visit to the school, they paid a visit to strength and conditioning Coach Todd Wright. As Wright examined Durant's physique and let him do some drills, he was amazed at his length and agility. It was something he had not seen before in his career. Here was a guy who was tall enough to be a center, had the body of a forward, and played like a full guard.

Durant reminded Wright of Longhorn's star T.J. Ford, who had led them to their most recent Final Four appearance. Durant jumped like his feet were on springs, causing Wright to say that Durant had a high-powered electrical system. The kid could practically soar 17.5 inches above the rim with one step. Wright called it repeat power. Although Wright saw some physical defects in Kevin, like the tightness in his ankles, back, and left hip, he knew that they were minimal and was excited to work with this unique specimen and make him even better. He knew the kid would develop into something special if he were properly worked on.

That night, Wright and some of the school's other coaches took father and son to a dinner at Ruth's Chris Steak House. As the group was watching an NBA playoff game on TV, Wayne Pratt noticed how Texas Longhorns Coach Rick Barnes wooed Kevin throughout the night. And just when Wright and Springman thought that Kevin would choose North Carolina because of its tradition, something happened.

Wayne Pratt tapped Wright's shoulders. He pointed to Kevin and Coach Barnes, who were deep in a serious conversation. When Durant and Barnes laughed hard at something they talked about, Pratt told Wright that he saw what he was looking for. Kevin Durant committed to the University of Texas that night.

Durant gained 10 pounds in his first two weeks in Austin. Wright, the conditioning coach who had examined him, designed a program to strengthen his weak spots and loosen his tight body parts. By the end of summer, Kevin Durant weighed a lean, but solid, 225 pounds. He was ready for college ball. When the Longhorns practiced at Cooley, Durant led fast breaks. He would finish them off with jump shots, drive with either hand, or dish off assist passes. He already looked like an All-American, and he had not played a single game yet. He was only 18 years old.

The Longhorns' season, though, started with uncertainty. The team had lost three of their big men from the previous season, and Barnes was left with three freshmen who could play inside -- Dexter Pittman, Matt Hill, and Kevin Durant. In his first exhibition game against Lenoir-Rhyne College, Kevin Durant got to a rough start by missing seven of his first eight shots. Durant said that he was nervous, but that was as bad as it got.

Less than two weeks later, Durant scored 20 points in his first collegiate game against Alcorn State at home on November 9, 2005. That was the highest scoring output for any freshman in Texas while playing his first game. There were only around four thousand spectators that night, fewer than half of the teams' season ticket holders. Sports fans were more interested in the

Rutgers-Louisville game that was on TV. Unfortunately for them, they missed out on the debut of a future NBA superstar. Durant's full arsenal was on display that night. He ran the breaks and finished with dunks. He made three-pointers – going three for six from behind the arc – and even dished off no-look passes. He also made six rebounds, three steals, and two blocks on the defensive end.

The audience came later as his legend grew when he scored 21 points in the next night against Chicago State in a 92-66 win on November 10, 2005, with more than 10 minutes extra on the floor. He was eight for 20 from the field and was nearly perfect from the free throw line with seven-for-eight baskets made. Defensively, he stood out with 12 of his 13 rebounds coming on the defensive end. Durant also added two assists, five blocks, and a steal.

Nearly a week later, Durant's minutes jumped to 39 in a close 63-61 loss to a powerhouse program in Michigan State in East Lansing, Michigan. Durant struggled from the field with only one three-point field goal out of eight attempts and 8-for-27 from the field overall. Texas would then bounce back with a 77-76 victory against St. John's Red Storm. Durant had a much better game with 29 points by shooting a 14-for-23 field goal rate in 32 minutes. He made five out of his six three-point shots while also collecting ten rebounds along with four assists and two blocks.

Durant was becoming a defensive nightmare for the other schools. He was too quick for the big men and too big for the faster but smaller players. On December 20, 2005, close to 12,000 spectators witnessed Durant drop 28 points against Arkansas. Most of those points came from inside the paint where Durant proved he can also score, aside from his outside bombs and fast break shots – all of which helped him shoot 10-for-16 from inside the three-point-line.

Then there was the Longhorns' ten-point loss to Gonzaga where Durant scored 29 points on perimeter shots, drives, jump hooks, and ten free throws. Coach Barnes was mad at Kevin Durant for settling for outside shots against the big players of Gonzaga. Barnes screamed at Durant and said, "Take him," referring to his bigger and slower defender. Barnes said no big man could guard Durant, and he was correct.

Rebounding was one of Kevin's strengths throughout the season. One of his best stretches in that statistic started in a December 28, 2005, win (76-66) over Centenary where Durant collected 17 rebounds (10 alone on the defensive side), along with his 21 points and three steals. Texas then defeated UT Arlington in an

84-52 victory at home where Durant scored another 21 points and had 12 of his 15 rebounds on defense. The rebounds would continue through the next few games – 16 rebounds at Colorado (102-78 win) on January 6, 2006; 13 rebounds vs. Missouri (88-68 win) on January 10, 2006; and 13 vs. Oklahoma (80-69 win) on January 13, 2006. He also had 12 rebounds in a tough 105-103 loss on-the-road at Oklahoma State on January 16, 2006.

Durant erupted for 37 points in Lubbock against Coach Bob Knight's methodical Texas Tech on January 31, 2006, in a 76-64 victory for the Longhorns. It was the third time in January that he scored 37 points. Durant scored 24 points in the second half, including 18 in the final eleven minutes as he made shots from virtually all over the court. Durant also grabbed a conference high of 23 rebounds. He blocked one shot and had three steals. After the game, Barnes bravely told reporters that it was the best performance of the year for the best player in the nation. Durant's collegiate career would be brief, but it was nonetheless spectacular.

Durant followed up with another 32 points in a February 3, 2006, loss back in Austin, to Kansas State with a score of 73-72. However, Durant does not go quietly in a loss. He shot nearly 62 percent within the three-point arc (making 13 for 21 attempts), another two out of four behind that line, and four out of five shots from the foul line. While Durant only had nine rebounds, he blocked five shots in another dominant defensive effort. The Longhorns would lose the next game on February 5, 2006, at Texas A&M (100-82). Durant had 28 points and 15 rebounds, although his accuracy was down with 13 for 31 for 41.9 percent. He missed 14 shots inside the three-point-line. Durant also had three assists, three steals, and three blocks.

At 16-7, entering the final stretch of the schedule, Durant and the Longhorns were hoping to get some momentum before the Big 12 Conference Championship tournament. They would accomplish that with a big six-game winning streak where Durant had four double-doubles. While Durant only scored 17 points and six rebounds on February 10, 2006, against Iowa State in a 77-68 win, he would see stronger games with 21 points and 12 rebounds on February 12, 2006, against Oklahoma State in an 83-54 revenge blowout.

Texas then earned a crucial road win against Baylor in Waco with a 68-67 win, thanks to Durant's 20 points in 40 minutes; although he had a lot of struggles from the field with less than 30 percent overall shooting from the field. However, he made his biggest plays on the defense – which he is known for – with 13 of his 14 total rebounds being defensive. Durant also had a couple of steals in that road win as well.

Durant's strongest games during the six-game stretch featured a 32-point performance on the road at Oklahoma in a 68-58 win on February 24, 2006, where he scored 70 percent of his field goal attempts – 9-for-14 inside, and five-for-six behind the three-point arc. Durant was also 9-for-10 from the free throw line. Durant also had ten rebounds, three blocks, and two steals.

A few nights later was one of Durant's toughest wins, a 98-96 overtime victory over Texas A&M on February 28, 2006, where he scored 30 points while shooting 52 percent. Durant also had 16 rebounds where, as seen in other games, the majority (11 to be exact) was collected while defending the basket. The streak was broken by Kansas on the road in a 90-86 loss where Durant still scored 32 points, nine rebounds, four steals, two blocks, and two assists.

While he was continuing to build his name as the Texas Longhorns' potential legend during the Big 12 Conference Championship tournament, Durant had some struggles in the opening round against Baylor on March 9, 2006, even though he scored 29 points in a 74-69 victory. His shooting percentage was 32 percent overall, and only two out of seven from the deep range behind the arc. However, he was nearly perfect with 11-for-13 free throws, and also had another good night on the boards with 13 rebounds in addition to four steals and three blocks.

Durant had a little more luck in the field goal percentage department with 26 points and eight rebounds and was 13-for-30 from the field in a 69-64 victory against Oklahoma State on March 10, 2006. Durant also had two steals to go along with a great game.

The Longhorns would lose in the conference championship game in an 88-84 loss on March 11, 2006, against the Kansas Jayhawks, despite Durant scoring 37 points – 10 came from his near-perfect performance on the free-throw line. Durant also had ten rebounds and six blocks to shine in front of the growing audiences who were becoming enamored with Durant.

Durant was given the Big 12 Tournament's Most Valuable Player award after scoring a tournament record of 92 points. Kevin Durant set a record for most points in a season with 903 points for both single-season school and Big 12. Durant's total of 390 rebounds was also a single-season school record, second in Big 12 history, and third all-time for a freshman in the history of the NCAA.

Despite not earning the automatic bid that comes with winning a conference tournament championship, Texas still received an at-large entry bid for the NCAA National Championship Tournament where legends like Larry Bird and Magic Johnson began to shine. Durant would debut with 27 points and eight rebounds in the Longhorns' 79-67 win on March 16, 2006, over New Mexico State, even though Durant struggled from the field with six-for-17 from the field. However, he was 15-for-16 from the foul line with three steals.

Durant and the Longhorns, however, were not able to advance to the NCAA Sweet 16 Round after losing 87-68 against the USC Trojans on March 18, 2006. Nevertheless, he still scored 30 points thanks to a 13 out of 33 overall field goal rate, six-for-eight from the line, and nine rebounds. In front of millions watching from home, Durant still had a couple of blocks and a steal on the defensive side of the court.

Durant was named National Player of the Year by the Associated Press, the National Basketball Association of Coaches (NBAC), the United States Basketball Writers Association (USBWA), CBS/Chevrolet, and the Sporting News.

Durant became the first ever freshman to win the Adolph Rupp Trophy, the Naismith Award, and the Wooden Award. Durant was also the third freshman after Wayman Tisdale (1983) and Chris Jackson (1989) to earn consensus First Team All-

American honors. Durant was named as Big 12 Freshman of the Year, Big 12 Player of the Year, earned First Team All-Conference honors, and was included in the Big 12's All-Defensive Team.

Looking over the entire season, Durant had plenty of success that was unmatched by any college basketball's usual freshman start. He scored 20-plus points 30 times and put up 30-plus points in 11 games. His career high was 37 points, which he accomplished on four occasions. Finally, his averages of 28.9 points and 12.5 rebounds in conference play were both single-season records for Big 12 league games.

With these record-breaking statistics, Durant was ready to take the leap to the National Basketball Association and maintain his young success beyond the Longhorn campus in Austin.

Chapter 4: Kevin's NBA Career

Getting Drafted

In April 2007, Durant held a news conference to announce that he would be leaving Texas after his freshman season to declare his eligibility for the NBA draft. Even during that conference, Durant's attire looked like he wanted to play basketball after facing the media. He was dressed in a Texas tank top and basketball shorts. His skinny arms were visible from his practice jersey as he sipped a sports drink. He talked like he was in a hurry to get back to the basketball court and join his teammates in the scrimmage.

Kevin Durant said that he thinks it was time to go, and that he was ready for his dream. It was not uncommon for basketball players to make the jump to the NBA after one year in college. It was not too long ago where players were able to declare their eligibility for the NBA Draft after graduating from high school at the age of 18. The final players to join after high school were in the 2005 NBA Draft, and included names like Andrew Bynum and Monta Ellis. However, in the later years, players being drafted out of high school were not meeting the same caliber as their predecessors, such as Kobe Bryant, Kevin Garnett, and LeBron James.

In the case of Durant, he was ready even before playing his first collegiate game. However, a new rule that required players to be at least 19 years old and out of high school for a year before entering the draft kept Durant out of the big league for a season. His wait before playing at the professional level falls into the traditional belief that all good things develop over time. After a successful season with the Longhorns, Durant was fully ready for the NBA

According to his mother, that one year made a huge difference for her son. Kevin matured as a person and player at Texas because the school took care of him. His Texas coach agreed. He said that everyone goes to college to better themselves. In the case of Durant, he said, he accomplished feats never before seen. With the decision to leave finalized, the only question for Durant was whether he would go to number one or number two.

Greg Oden was also a freshman sensation at Ohio State. Like Durant, he had phenomenal credentials. He led his high school team to an eye-popping 103-7 record and took his Ohio State Buckeyes to the National Title game with a 35-4 record. Oden was a fan favorite whose personality was like Shaquille O'Neal. His game was also as dominant as the Big Diesel. He averaged 15.7 points, 9.6 rebounds, and 3.3 blocks, and was efficient because he took few shots to score so many points. Like Shaq, he was dominant in the paint, but unlike O'Neal, he had soft hands and ran the floor very well. At 7 feet and 260 pounds, he was the ideal center to build a team around and win championships with. Oden's name was said in the same breath as Russell, Chamberlain, Abdul-Jabbar, and O'Neal. Nevertheless, Kevin Durant was not the typical player to pass on in the draft.

Similar to Oden, Durant was a physical specimen as well. During the pre-draft measurements, he was reported to be 6'9" without his shoes on. When he had his sneakers on, he would shoot up to more than 6'10".[i] For a young man that played guard plenty of times in college, Durant's size at the perimeter was something to behold. Durant was also measured with a 7'5" wingspan that made him virtually unguardable when shooting the ball. If Oden had a chance to become the second coming of Shaq because of his size, Durant had the opportunity to become his own unique legend given his height and length for a perimeter player.

Often compared to the likes of Dirk Nowitzki and Tracy McGrady, Kevin Durant was a combination of the two All-Star players as far as physical attributes and skills were concerned. Like Dirk, he was tall and long, but could shoot over defenders from the perimeter. Similar to T-Mac, KD was a big player that could move and handle the ball like smaller guards could. And like the two All-Stars, Durant was a matchup nightmare because of his size and wide array of skills.

Regarding skills, Kevin Durant was a polished offensive force. He handled the ball like guards do and could even break defenses with his ability to dribble drive and finish with flair and grace at the rim, if not with the force his athleticism gives him. On transition, his length and running speed make him look like a gazelle that could travel coast to coast in two seconds. His game at the low post, though not as polished as his other skills, were also already impressive enough for his age.[ii]

Shooting-wise, Durant probably had no equal in his draft class. At the size of 6'10", Kevin Durant could look like a shooting guard whenever he comes off screens for catch-and-shoot situations. His three-point accuracy, in college, was also excellent as his range already seemed fit for the NBA distance. And while his distant shots were consistent weapons for him, he did most of his damage on the mid-range.[ii]

Durant, on the perimeter, has shown himself to be an unstoppable scoring machine. Given his length, he could shoot over defenders from midrange and has not demonstrated any trouble making those shots in catch-and-shoot situations whether contested or uncontested. And even with the ball in his hands out on the perimeter, Durant already had all the skills to create open situations for himself. Since he could handle the ball like a guard, Kevin Durant could open enough distance between him and his defenders to rise and make unguardable jump shots.[ii]

In the other aspects of the game, Durant certainly knows well enough how to use his length and size to grab rebounds. He was an excellent rebounder in college despite playing a perimeter position. Kevin Durant's hops and long arms certainly help him grab rebounders that he could not normally get his hands on. If he puts all of his effort in that facet, he could become a great rebounder in the NBA.

Kevin Durant was also ready for the NBA as far as the intangibles were concerned. He was never hesitant in scoring the ball, and it seemed like he was born with the scoring mentality that only a few other players in the history of the game has ever had. He has the confidence needed to become a go-to guy in the league and has also shown a great feel for the game that is worthy of an All-Star. Concerning his leadership skills, a young Kevin Durant matured well enough for his age when he saw competition in the NCAA Tournament as the teenage leader of Texas. With all that said and done, Durant has all the physical gifts, skills, and qualities that could turn him into a once-in-a-lifetime basketball talent.

Simply looking at Kevin Durant and what he could do on the court would lead one to think that he was a lock for the top spot in the 2007 NBA Draft. However, there were still arguments against the long and tall freshman from Texas. As good as he already was and as transcendent a college player and future NBA star as Durant was, he still had several weaknesses to his game.

Physically, Kevin Durant may be tall, long, and athletic, but he was skinny for his size and his position. Measuring below 220 pounds coming into the draft, Durant looked like a long twig compared to the matured frames and bodies that his peers were sporting. On top of all that, Durant was never really a strong player. In the pre-draft workouts, he could not even bench press 185 pounds and had a severe hatred towards strength training even back in his younger years as a player. Despite being bigger and longer than almost all of the players in the draft class, Durant was the only player that could not bench 185 pounds.[iii] That meant that even the tiny point guards were arguably stronger than he was. If KD wanted to shed the notion that he could probably become a bust because of his severe lack of strength, he needed to bulk up and become stronger.

Though Kevin Durant did not have a lot of weakness in his offensive game, the one major flaw in his attack plan was always his tendency to avoid contact when going up against the defenders inside the paint. The reason was most probably because of his lack of upper body strength and size to absorb and finish through contact. Other than that, Durant already seemed like a complete offensive package.

Durant's transcendent abilities in scoring may have sometimes also become his weakness. KD attracts so much defensive attention that opposing teams tend to focus their defensive strategies on him. When doubled, Kevin Durant seemed frustrated and confused at times, and it often led to bad possessions. His lack of a superior court vision and passing instincts tend to compound that problem. While not necessarily a bad passer, Durant has often focused too much on scoring that his passing skills have yet to be fully developed and realized.[ii]

Defense was not also one of the best attributes that Kevin Durant sported coming into the NBA Draft. On paper, KD had the foot speed and wingspan to become an elite defender on any level of basket. However, the mentality, patience, and timing were still off as he is yet to become a lockdown defender. And with his length and height, one would expect him to become a solid shot blocker.

The Portland Trail Blazers owned the top pick in the 2007 NBA Draft. Although they had two ultra-talented college freshmen to choose from, the general manager at the time, Kevin Pritchard, said that it was the most difficult decision he had to make. Comparing Durant and Oden was not easy, much like comparing apples to apples. Oden was a physical specimen and an athletic freak, while Durant was a complete all-around player who was a scoring machine.

As the draft drew closer, the comparisons and debate on who between the two promising and talented players was the better top overall pick only became hotter and hotter. Kevin Durant was a once-in-a-lifetime talent, especially when it came to putting the ball through the hoop. Meanwhile, Greg Oden had all the makings to develop into an elite center in the league. The debate went all the way back to 1984 when the Houston Rockets were contemplating who to pick for the top spot in the draft. It was a choice between Hakeem Olajuwon and Michael Jordan.

The Rockets were not wrong in drafting Hakeem "The Dream." He went on to become a multiple-time All-Star, a two-time NBA champion, an MVP, a Defensive Player of the Year, a two-time Finals MVP, the best shot blocker in NBA history, and arguably the most fundamentally sound center the league has ever seen. However, it was also painful for them to pass out on Michael Jordan, who would win six NBA titles, ten scoring championships, five MVP's, and become the best player in all of basketball history. While Oden and Durant were nowhere near Olajuwon and Jordan at that point in their lives, both of them had the potential to get there.

Meanwhile, the Portland Trailblazers were also trying to move on from the stigma of that 1984 NBA Draft when they chose Sam Bowie, who was marred by injuries early on in his career, instead of Michael Jordan. They had all the chances to pick the man that would become the "Greatest of All Time," but chose not to because they had a player in Clyde Drexler, who played a similar style as Jordan did. Nevertheless, the 2007 NBA Draft would become another turning point in franchise history. Would they pick another Bowie in the making? Or were they destined to choose a man of Jordan's caliber?

The argument for picking Greg Oden as the top overall pick was just as convincing as choosing Kevin Durant for that spot. Oden is a large athlete. He is 7-feet tall and weighs nearly 270 pounds of solid muscle for a young gun. Greg Oden is also an athletic freak that could demolish any other center with his strength and explosiveness under the basket.

Physically, Oden was just as impressive, if not more impressive, than Durant was coming into the draft. But Oden was not just a simple physical beast. He was also a talented center on both ends of the floor. Offensively, Greg Oden had soft hands that helped him hit hook shots and turnaround jumpers at the low post. While he is capable of hitting the kind of delicate finesse shots that Shaquille O'Neal could never do, he could also power his way for easy baskets much like Shaq did back in the day. As he connected over 60% of his shots while averaging a double-double in college, Greg Oden surely had the makings of an efficient double-double machine in the NBA.

While Greg Oden was just as promising an offensive talent as Kevin Durant was, the aspect he excels far ahead of KD was at the defensive end of the court. Oden was a defensive monster even back when he was winning titles in high school. He had good, mobile feet that helped him in recovering to protect the basket. He also had good timing when it came to going up to block shots at the rim. And in one-on-one situations, he excelled at defending opposing centers and even frustrated them so much that he was often proclaimed an offensively better version of Bill Russell.[iv]

With what Greg Oden could bring to the table as a promising big man that could even become the second coming of a

Hakeem Olajuwon with the strength and size of Shaq, there was no reason to wonder why a lot of analysts were still choosing him over Kevin Durant. This was despite all of the latter's once-in-a-generation combination of length and supreme scoring prowess. Nevertheless, both prospects had all the potential to become franchise superstars.

On draft day, Durant could not believe his agent when he told him that Portland was picking Oden. Durant had already envisioned how good the Blazers would be with him playing alongside Brandon Roy and LaMarcus Aldridge. Though the Blazers were also keen on what KD could bring to the table, they needed a defensive big man that could cover the basket and help proven players like Zach Randolph and Roy. So when then Commissioner David Stern officially made Greg Oden the number one pick, Kevin Durant was headed to Seattle SuperSonics at number two.

Rookie Season

Durant knew little about Seattle other than hearing the latest news that they had traded Ray Allen to Boston and were about to deal Rashard Lewis to the Orlando Magic. Rookie General Manager Sam Presti had watched Durant play for the Texas Longhorns and knew he was going to be an elite scorer. It was pretty apparent that the Sonics' management was clearing the roster to hand over the team keys to Kevin Durant, which is a risky move for any professional sports franchise.

After a few months, Presti would realize he was lucky that the Blazers picked Oden. Apparently, Pritchard's pick in Portland became another big man tragedy for the Blazers after Bill Walton and Sam Bowie. Oden missed his rookie season with a knee injury that would hound him for the rest of his career. Greg Oden was another Bowie to the Blazers, who missed out on their chance to grab a Jordan-esque scoring prodigy like Kevin Durant. On the other hand, in Seattle, a storm was about to be unleashed.

With news of Greg Oden's injury flooding the league, Kevin Durant was about to be named the consensus pick for the Rookie of the Year award even though he was yet to play his first NBA game. There was no indeed no question that KD was going to become the best freshman in the NBA that season, especially since he was going to be tasked to carry the offensive load for a rebuilding Sonics team.

At only 19 years old, Durant was the lone offensive bright spot of the Seattle SuperSonics, who had a team full of role-playing veterans playing together with the young star from Texas and an equally promising rookie forward Jeff Green. With guys like Nick Collison, Earl Watson, and Chris Wilcox unable to put the ball through the hoop regularly, Kevin Durant was going to become the entire offensive attack of the Sonics in just his rookie season.

In Durant's first game in the NBA, the SuperSonics lost 120-103 on October 31, 2006, in Denver. Durant scored only 18 points after shooting 31 percent from the field, with seven field goals, and only five rebounds on defense. He would then make a personal bounce back by torching the Phoenix Suns for 27 points on 11 out of 23 shooting from the field. Nevertheless, the Sonics lost that one before losing a third consecutive game to the Clippers when Durant scored 24 on 10 out of 19 shooting from the floor. In his fourth game of the season, KD would score 27 again as he shot 11 out of 22 against Sacramento. However, the Sonics would lose four straight games. They would eventually open the season with an eight-game losing streak.

For the first time in his professional career, Kevin Durant would experience the sweet taste of an NBA victory in his ninth game in the league. Against the Miami Heat on November 14, Durant had 18 points despite a tough shooting night to upset the defending champions of two seasons ago. He would then help his team win back-to-back when he had 21 points against the Atlanta Hawks two days later.

After several games hovering between the 15-25 point range, Durant would score 35 points for the first time in a 95-93 win on November 30, against the Indiana Pacers in Seattle. It was one of Durant's best shooting performances as a professional with 60 percent of his field goals scoring points, including three out of five from behind the three-point arc. Durant also collected five rebounds on defense along with two steals and three blocks. At 19 years old, KD became the second youngest player ever to score at least 30 points in a game. Only LeBron James was younger than him in that regard. From then on, scoring above 30 points would become a personal habit for Kevin Durant, the scoring prodigy.

Durant would score 35 points again on December 12, 2006, during a 104-98 home victory over the Milwaukee Bucks – 15 of which came from the free-throw line, while also shooting 9-for-20 from the field (45 percent). Durant also collected eight rebounds and showed some of the defense that had made him famous back in Austin, Texas, with five blocked shots.

Durant would score beyond the 30-point mark four more times, including a performance where he scored 37 points and eight defensive rebounds during a very high-scoring 151-147 home victory against the Denver Nuggets on April 6, 2007. It was a game where Durant was perfect shooting from the free throw line with 13 total foul shots while also going 11 out of 24 from the field for just under 50 percent to go along with nine assists – very close to a triple-double – and three steals.

Throughout the season, Kevin Durant was also an unchallenged rookie out in the Western Conference where things tend to be tougher in the NBA. Out of the six months that he played in the regular season, he was Western Conference Rookie of the Month five times. The only time he did not win the award was in February when veteran rookie Luis Scola won it. That simply shows how matured of an offensive player Durant already was in just his first season in the league.

Kevin Durant, in another highlight of the season, also showed his mettle against players a little older and more experienced that he was. In the 2008 Rising Stars Challenge, KD was the leader of the rookie team that went toe-to-toe with the sophomore squad. Despite losing to the more experienced group, Durant proved once again that he was the best freshman in the NBA when he led the rookies with 23 points and eight rebounds in that exhibition game.

Kevin Durant's best game was the final game of the season on April 16, 2007, on-the-road for a 126-121 victory where Durant had a 42-point game with 13 rebounds, six assists, two blocks, and one steal to finish a spectacular rookie season where he averaged 20.3 points, 4.4 rebounds, and 2.4 assists. He was the first rookie to average more than 20 points in a game since Carmelo Anthony (21) and LeBron James (20.9). And, joining the same two players, KD also became the third teenager to score at least 20 points per game in his rookie season. He also became the first rookie to lead his team in scoring, like Emeka Okafor and Josh Childress did in 2004-2005.

As Durant won these accolades, he was knocked to his knees all year long. He was often criticized for flopping too much. However, the truth was that he was not strong enough to stay on his feet to defend heftier opponents. There were rumors that he could not even bench press 185 pounds, much less than the 225 pounds he weighed in at during his freshman year with the Texas Longhorns the prior year because all he ate was chicken and candies. He was called "Starvin'" and "String Bean" by his buddies because of his reed-thin 215-pound frame. Durant was so thin that Sonics Coach P.J. Carlesimo played him as a six-foot-nine guard at that time.

Durant was also labeled a "chucker" because he took 1,366 shots from the field and made just 43 percent. He was just taking orders from Carlesimo, who tasked him to shoot and shoot some more. GM Presti would make sure to walk Kevin out of the arena to check his spirits because so much pressure was put on Durant's lean shoulders. Durant would later silence his early critics by winning the 2007 Rookie of the Year award, beating the Hawks' Al Horford. Thus, he became the first, and possibly the last, in Seattle's franchise history to win such honor for the Emerald City.

Despite being far ahead of Horford regarding statistics and impact, Kevin Durant failed to convince several voters to give him first place votes for the Rookie of the Year award though he would still win it. Al Horford had a solid first season but was not impressive compared to the numbers and the abilities that Durant was already showing. If anything, Kevin Durant should have won that award unanimously as he was certainly head and shoulders above the rest of the rookie class that season despite being only 19 years old.

However, though Durant was having considerable personal success, the Sonics were floundering. The team struggled and had the worst record in franchise history with 20 wins, while off-court battles were being waged on where the team would play in the future.

Continued Rise, Pairing Up With Russell Westbrook

The Sonics were relocated to Oklahoma City in 2009 as part of the settlement that called on owner Clay Bennett to pay the city an estimated $75 million in exchange for the immediate termination of the lease of Key Arena. As part of the deal, Seattle retained the team name "SuperSonics," the team logo, and colors for a possible future NBA team.

Bennett purchased the Sonics in 2006 from Starbucks mogul Howard Schultz for $350 million on the presumption that he wanted to move the franchise. A lawsuit followed after Schultz sought to regain ownership and control of the team. He alleged that Bennett did not follow through on their agreement to negotiate in good faith for the construction of a new arena in Seattle, one year before trying to relocate the team to another city. Bennett won the legal battles, and the team was moved to his hometown of Oklahoma City. Kevin Durant would become the face of his second franchise – not the way many NBA legends had done in the past, though it is no fault of his own.

On Durant's first day as a Thunder player, the team opened its first practice to the public. But before that, Presti took the team to the site of the Oklahoma City bombings on its 13th year anniversary. The bombing is one of the biggest tragedies in American history. Timothy McVeigh and Terry Nichols masterminded the bomb attack that killed 168 people at the Oklahoma City Federal Building.

With the city's reputation tied to the bloodbath and the bombing, the citizens of Oklahoma City spent the next ten years voting for sales taxes to renovate the downtown area. About $125 million of that revenue was set aside to transform their arena into an NBA standard arena.

Durant had seen the bomb site before as a University of Texas student, but he was almost overcome with emotions when he and the Thunder walked through the memorial ground. He said right there and then, he wanted to go to the gym right away and do something that the city would be proud of. During their first practice, they were mobbed by cheering fans looking for new heroes. The bond was immediately created.

When the season started, the Thunders were on pace to becoming the worst team in NBA history after starting 3-29, but the fans kept filling the arena to cheer them on. When they arrived in town, Presti said he was told that the new city put a premium on substance over style. That was Kevin Durant, and that was why he immediately settled into his new city.

Durant was in local churches, and he thanked God for the opportunity to play basketball every day. The fans saw him pray at the scorer's table, high-five with kids at courtside, and hug his mother after each game. When his brother, godfather, and father came to watch him, he would also hug them after the match. With everything going for him off the court, the only problem for Durant was how to translate that into wins.

Durant worked harder. He would come to the gym 90 minutes before the shoot-around practices to take 100 shots and lift weights. He would even eat breakfast at the facility and treat the shoot-around practices like a real game. The gym became his own, and much like the young Kevin of the Saint Pleasant Recreation Center, Durant worked harder and harder. Durant's diet also changed from chicken and candies to pancakes, waffles, turkey bacon, and sausages for breakfast, and then baked chicken, fish, and stir fry for lunch. He was determined to become a stronger physical presence on the court and build up to a more substantial weight like he had back in Texas. As a result of this ultimate dedication, head coach Scott Brooks once called Durant boring because his home was the basketball court. It was boring indeed, but it was a "good" boring.

On the court, Durant had a slow start with only 12 points and three rebounds in the season opening at home against Milwaukee on October 29, 2008, in a 98-87 loss. Three days later, Durant started getting back into his groove with 26 points, five rebounds, and four steals on November 1, 2008, against the Houston Rockets – although it was another loss with a score of 89-77.

For most of the start of the early season, Kevin Durant still seemed like another version of his rookie self. He was still inconsistent from the field as he was trying to find his offensive groove at that early part of the year. He would shoot above 50% only one in his first six games of the season as he was looking like a one-hit-wonder bust. But Durant would steadily prove himself as a supreme young talent.

Kevin Durant would finally break through the 30-point barrier that season after torching the Indiana Pacers defense for 37 points on 13 out of 27 shooting. He also had eight rebounds and three blocks in that game, which saw the OKC Thunder losing their sixth game in seven tries. It would take a little longer until the Thunder would snap the losing culture that hounded them at that early part of the season.

Durant would score exactly 30 points two more times in November – during a November 22, 2008, road game against the New Orleans Hornets, and November 29, 2008, against the Memphis Grizzlies on-the-road for only the Thunder's second win of the season. That win against the Grizzlies snapped the 13-game losing streak for the Thunder. Nevertheless, they were still a laughable team at that point in the season.

On October 5, KD would have his first double-double of the year as he scored 16 points and collected ten rebounds in a loss to the Magic. Three days later, Durant would surpass the 40-point scoring mark for the first time of the season with 41 points in a losing effort at home against the Golden State Warriors (112-102). For his second double-double performance, he had ten rebounds on the defensive side of the court to go along with three blocked shots and one steal.

Offensively, Kevin Durant found a sense of consistency during December when he was continuously putting up 20 or more points on respectable shooting clips from the field. He was also playing the other aspects of the game better as he was seen collecting 13 rebounds while scoring 28 points in a loss to the

Spurs on December 14. And though the Oklahoma City Thunder were still losing, the fact that most of their losses were hard-fought games meant that they were improving.

To end the year 2008 right, Kevin Durant had one of the best all-around performances he had put up at that young stage of his career when his Thunder defeated the Warriors on December 31. He had 25 points on 9 out of 18 shooting while also collecting ten rebounds and six assists in that winning effort. And though he would lose in his first game in the year 2009, he did have 33 points, nine rebounds, and five assists while nearly beating the Denver Nuggets.

The theme for Kevin Durant in that first month of the new calendar year was that he was putting more efforts on the rebounding end after merely averaging less than five boards in his rookie season. While still continuing his scoring rampages, Durant was grabbing rebounds at an excellent rate as he had six double-double performances in January after collecting double-digit rebounds only four times in the last two months.

One of Durant's strongest overall games came in a close 107-104 loss on the road to the Los Angeles Clippers on January 23, 2009, where Durant had a new career best of 46 points and 15 rebounds – 13 came off the defensive glass. Once again, Durant was a double-double machine as he continued the same effort of rebounding the ball even after focusing more on scoring the basket. A good portion of his points in that game came from the free throw line where he made 24 out of 26.

That career game for Kevin Durant helped him and his team win the next two games to go for five wins in their last seven games. In that second win, which was against the Memphis Grizzlies, he had 35 points, ten rebounds, and six assists in an overtime outing for the Thunder. He would then end January with a double-double in a loss to the Utah Jazz.

While Kevin Durant was seen piling up double-double performances in January, his February saw him upping up the ante concerning scoring. He would start the month by scoring 33 points in an overtime loss to the Sacramento Kings. He made 13 out of 23 attempts from the field in that game. After that match, KD would score at least 30 points in the next four games, which included three 31-point performances and a lone 39-point outing.

After his 30-point streak ended with a 20-point effort in a loss to the Trailblazers on February 11, Kevin Durant would return to the All-Star Weekend as a participant in the Rising Stars Challenge. This time, he was part of the winning sophomore team. After proving that he was indeed the best rookie a year ago in the same event, KD would make the NBA coaches regret the decision of not voting him for the All-Star team after he scored 46 points. He broke the record which was previously held by Amar'e Stoudemire and won the Rising Stars Challenge Most Valuable Player award.

After the All-Star break, Durant would use his MVP momentum to put up another show and be the star that shines in another losing effort by scoring 47 points in a 100-98 loss to the New Orleans Hornets on February 17, 2008. Durant made nearly 60 percent of his shots from the field, including 4 of 6 from behind the three-point line.

After another career scoring performance from Kevin Durant, the high-scoring second-year forward would score at least 30 points three more times for the month of February. In that entire calendar month, Durant would only score less than 30 twice. The first one was when he had 20 points against Portland, and the second was when he scored 6 point after playing only seven minutes due to a severely sprained ankle in a game against the Dallas Mavericks on February 27.

Kevin Durant would miss a total of seven games due to the ankle injury. He would make his return to the OKC Thunder lineup on March 14 to score 22 points in a loss. Though Durant was still putting up good scoring numbers after his return from injury, it was clear that his momentum was cut off and that the ankle was still probably bothering him since he was not able to replicate the performances he had in January and in February.

It was an overall good sophomore year in the NBA for Durant, who finished with 15 double-doubles and an average of 25.8 points per game, with a season shooting accuracy of 47.6 percent. He also averaged 6.5 rebounds and nearly three assists per game. After improving his scoring average by five points, Durant was a strong candidate for the Most Improved Player award. He finished third in the voting.

Despite the Thunder's struggles with a slightly improved 23-59 record to return to the cellar of the Western Conference's Northwest Division, the team's young star had another solid year of development. His season's impressive numbers could be credited to Durant pressing Brooks to make him play all 48 minutes so the team could win. While Brooks said that he would have loved to oblige, he joked with Durant that Presti would fine him if he did so. Durant would reply to Brooks that he would pay the fine.

And though the Thunder did not seem like any threat for the majority of that season, they were about to become a dangerous young force in the NBA after finding their groove and chemistry in the latter part of that long six-month battle. Kevin Durant's improvements can be credited for their rise as a young team. But what was equally important was the fact that the Thunder had seen potential in Russell Westbrook, who they drafted fifth overall in the 2008 NBA Draft.

Westbrook, who played shooting guard for UCLA, quickly adjusted to the point guard position with the Thunder, though he was obviously still struggling with the nuances needed of a playmaker. Despite not being the prototypical pass-first point guard, Westbrook was the one that eased the burden off Kevin Durant as he was also a capable scorer by being ultra-quick and athletic at the backcourt position.

While Kevin Durant provided the scoring touch and leadership for the OKC Thunder, Russell Westbrook was the Energizer bunny that gave the team the battery they needed whenever they looked lethargic. Russ was not only very quick and athletic, but was also a high-energy hustle player that had just as much confidence as Kevin Durant. Though he was and would often be criticized for his knack of putting up a lot of shots and taking away possessions from KD, he and Durant would form the deadliest duo the NBA has ever seen in that era of basketball.

Focusing on Kevin Durant, Scott Brooks would say that he's never seen a sophomore player try to lead his team this hard since Magic Johnson did for the Lakers. Durant was a natural leader, and he led by example with his hard work, which also stretched beyond the basketball court and into the surrounding community.

Durant returned to his roots and donated $25,000 to the Saint Pleasant Recreation Center. The donation built a game room for the kids at the facility, and it included an X-box, a 55-inch TV, and plush couches that kids could sleep on in case they had nowhere to go. He also went back to Barry Farms D.C. to play exhibition games with other NBA players. After a summer of fulfillment during which he was able to go home and revisit his past, Kevin Durant returned for his third NBA season as a man on a mission.

First All-Star Season and Scoring Title, Trip to the Playoffs

The 2009-10 season would become the turning point not only for Kevin Durant as an individual player, but the entire Oklahoma City Thunder organization. For KD, the brilliant season would start off with a regimen that saw him training his strength more than he ever did in his young career. He was just off a season from nearly being an All-Star, but still needed a lot more work to get to the level of a legitimate franchise player.

KD would first seek the services of Alan Stein, a strength and conditioning coach Durant met back when he was still in high school. Stein was a legend back in Durant's hometown as he was known for working out with some of the best basketball talents in that side of the country. His goal for KD was simple. Stein wanted the young star to strengthen his major muscle groups while minimizing his risk of injury. Kevin Durant would start to feel the difference of the strength training and would pack a little bit of weight over the offseason.[v] Despite still being lean, Durant was far off from the weak twig he was in his rookie season.

For the Oklahoma City Thunder, the start of the improvements began with the work that both Kevin Durant and Russell Westbrook went through during the offseason. The Thunder were also lucky enough to have made good offseason moves that made their roster better. And similar to how they acquired KD and Russ, the OKC front office did their homework for the NBA Draft.

The Thunder, because of their bad record in the 2008-09 regular season, were able to get the third overall pick in the 2009 NBA Draft. The class of 2009 was a stacked one. It featured consensus top overall pick Blake Griffin and shot blocking expert Hasheem Thabeet, who were slated to be chosen as the first and second overall draftees that season. From the third pick onwards, the choices were going to have to boil down to franchise needs rather than pure talent. Nevertheless, even the lower lottery choices were still very much talented as youngsters like James Harden, Tyreke Evans, Ricky Rubio, Stephen Curry, DeMar DeRozan, and Brandon Jennings, among others were up for grabs.

Among those several other talented draft choices, the favorite to go number three in the draft was the phenomenal Spanish point guard Rubio. Curry, who was the nation's leading scorer in college was also seen as a good choice for the Thunder. However, the Oklahoma City Thunder were already high on their converted point guard Russell Westbrook, who showed promise as Durant's running mate. They did not need another point guard.

Realizing that they needed a third man that could relieve pressure off of their rising duo, the Thunder decided to draft James Harden out of Arizona. Harden was one of the craftiest shooting guards in college back in his second year with Arizona. He was also a proven shooter from behind the arc. It was an ability that Scott Brooks needed to space the floor for his two best players. Other than that, Brooks also needed Harden to lead the Thunder second unit while his duo of rising stars was on the bench resting.

The Thunder, to finally complete their young core stars that could complement the franchise player Kevin Durant, signed 6'10" athletic shot blocker Serge Ibaka, who they drafted back in 2008 near the end of that season's draft. The addition of Harden and Ibaka to the team would make the Oklahoma City Thunder arguably the scariest young team in the NBA. Though they were seen as a developing squad that would not make the playoffs anytime sooner, Kevin Durant would have something to say about that as the 2009-10 season kicked off.

While Durant's breakout improvement season already came in his second year with the Thunder, it was during his third year when his transformation into a legitimate superstar was finally realized. The NBA would soon feel and see the full force of what Durant could do as a transcendent scorer and as rising star that still had room to grow.

He started the season with back-to-back 25-point double-double games in wins against the Sacramento Kings and the Detroit Pistons. While he would hover around his usual sophomore numbers during the first few games of the season when the Thunder seemed to have gone back to their losing ways, Durant would start the tear on November 10, 2009, when he would score 37 points on the Sacramento Kings.

After putting up 30 and 25 points respectively versus the LA Clippers and the San Antonio Spurs in wins for the Thunder, it would not take long for Kevin Durant to break the 40-point barrier when he had 40 points in a losing effort to the Clips in just his 10th game that season. He made 14 of his 25 shots and converted 10 of his 11 free throw attempts in that match. He would bounce back by scoring 32 on the Miami Heat when the Thunder won their next game.

Kevin Durant would then put up phenomenal scoring performances for the month of December of that season. He started it off by scoring 33 points in a win versus the Philadelphia 76ers and finishing three of his next five games scoring at least 30 points. He barely missed the 30-point mark when he went toe-to-toe with future rival LeBron James when the Thunder lost to the Cavs on December 13. He had 29 points while LeBron finished with 44 to get the better of the inexperienced youngster. But those performances were not the best scoring stretch he experienced that month. It would take a challenge from one of his childhood idols to finally turn him into the scoring demon that he was.

In a game against no less than one of his favorite players on December 22, Kevin Durant and his Thunder would try and challenge the defending champions, the Los Angeles Lakers, led by Kobe Bryant, one of the best scorers the league has ever seen. Not willing to back down from the Black Mamba himself, KD would try to match Kobe's production that night in a close game. He would score 30 points on 11 out of 19 shooting. However, his idol got the best of him as Kobe finished with 40 points and the win in that game.

After that loss to Kobe and the Lakers, Kevin Durant tapped into a side of him the league has never seen before from the third-year rising forward. Versus the Phoenix Suns on December 23, he had 38 points on a 60% shooting clip to beat the Nash-led team. He would then help the Thunder win their next four games by doing what he does best—putting the ball through the hoop.

The Thunder would beat the Bobcats with Durant scoring 30 points before he would put up 40 in a blowout win against the

New Jersey Nets. KD made almost 70% of his shots in that game. In a match against his hometown crowd in Washington, Kevin Durant would torch the Wizards for 35 points along with 11 rebounds and four assists. He would finish the winning streak with 31 points on the Jazz before ending his personal 30-point scoring stretch with 31 points once again in a loss to the Bucks on January 2, 2010. In the fifteen games he played in December, Durant averaged nearly 30 points that month.

On January 9, 2010, Durant would help the Thunder defeat the Pacers at home in a 108-102 victory with 40 points off of 66.7 percent shooting from the field – he hit both of his three-point shots and was 14-for-16 from the foul line. All 12 rebounds in that game came while playing defense. That was his third 40-point game that season. He would then score 30 or more points in the next four games after that eruption.

While Kevin Durant was offensively explosive in the month of December, he was an even better scorer in January of 2010. He averaged 32 points in January while scoring at least 30 points in all but four of the 15 games he played that month. His best performance for January came at the end of the month when he lit the Golden State Warriors up with 45 points. He made 16 of his 21 shots while also converting all of his 11 free throw attempts. KD also grabbed 11 rebounds that game.

While he was scoring more than 2,400 points on the season, Durant would also make his mark with his continued ability to collect rebounds off the opposing teams' missed opportunities. The most defensive rebounds he had in one single game came in a 99-98 loss visiting the Dallas Mavericks on January 15, 2010, a game where he had 13 off the defending glass as well as one steal. On a side note, Durant scored 30 points in that game as well.

With the way Kevin Durant was lighting up the NBA landscape with his unreal ability to score the basketball from all angles and any distance, the third-year forward and leading scorer of the league was awarded his first ever All-Star Game. Despite not starting, Durant converted 15 points in 20 minutes in his first appearance in the midseason classic.

Kevin Durant continued his scoring tear even after he had already proven himself as an All-Star. Fresh off the break, he had 25 points and 14 rebounds to lead the OKC Thunder to their sixth straight victory. He would then have at least 30 points in the next three games to push the Thunder streak to nine wins, which were their highest since relocating to Oklahoma City.

Later in March of that year, Kevin Durant would score 45 points for the second time that season. In that loss to the San Antonio

Spurs, KD shot 15 of 24 from the field and 14 of 15 from the free throw line. A few weeks later, just when the season was about to end, Durant had back-to-back 40-point games for the first time in his career.

In that April 4 game against the Minnesota Timberwolves, KD had 40 points on 13 of 22 shooting from the field to push the Thunder closer to solidifying the final spot in the Western Conference playoff picture. Two days later, he dropped 45 on the Utah Jazz, converting seven three-pointers in that narrow loss. He would then score at least 30 points in the next five games, one of which saw him scoring 40 for the eighth time that season. The final scoring stretch from Durant not only helped the Thunder earn the eighth seed in the West, but it also helped KD hold on to the scoring lead he had over LeBron James that season.

Despite being paired up with the Kobe Bryant-led Los Angeles Lakers in the first round of the Western Conference playoffs, the Thunders took the Lakers to six games before losing the series 4-2. In Durant's NBA playoff debut, the Thunder lost 87-79 on April 18, 2010, where he scored 24 points but only made about 29 percent of his field goals. He was 9-for-11 from the free throw line.

After falling 2-0 in the series, the Thunders would win their first two games in Oklahoma City to tie the series with a 101-96 win on April 22, 2010, where Durant scored 29 points and collected 19 rebounds. They then had a 110-89 win on April 24, 2010, where Durant scored 22 points with four rebounds and two blocked shots.

However, the Lakers would close out the series and eventually move on to win the NBA Finals in seven games against the Boston Celtics. At the end of his third NBA season, Durant became a candidate for the league's Most Improved Player of the Year award, which was eventually given to Danny Granger of the Indiana Pacers.

Despite the early playoffs exit, Durant's continued improvement as the leader of the Oklahoma City franchise would begin to pay off the next season. Durant lit up the league by averaging 30.1 points per game to become the youngest-ever scoring champion in the history of the NBA at 21. Durant would be named to his first All-NBA selection, and the Thunder won 27 more games than the previous season. The team would defy conventional odds and reach the playoffs.

It was not only the team's success that defined Durant's third season. There was this road game against the Utah Jazz with playoff positioning on the line, and the Thunder trailed 139-140 with just a couple of seconds left to play in the match. As Durant launched a three-pointer, he was apparently hacked by CJ Miles. However, referee Tony Bothers did not blow his whistle as Durant missed the shot. Instead of getting mad at the referee, Durant told reporters after the game that the play was not a foul because the refs did not call one. That was it, a simple reply that left GM Presti saying that this was the kind of attitude that the organization had always preached. That was how the team wanted to do things in Oklahoma City. It defined Durant's character and class as a player.

The All-Star Partnership with Russell Westbrook, Reaching the Conference Finals

The offseason followed LeBron's *The Decision* summer, and while James, Wade, and Bosh made a lot of fanfare with the Big Three combination in Miami, Kevin Durant quietly became one of the world's premier players. Durant led Team USA to the gold medal in the 2010 World Championships to re-establish the Americans' dominance of the game. Durant averaged a stunning 22 points per game and was named as Tournament MVP. At that time, Oklahoma City and Durant were negotiating a contract extension which would keep him in OKC for the next five years.

On the same day that LeBron went to ESPN to announce that he would be taking his talents to South Beach, Kevin Durant tweeted that he had re-signed with the Thunder for approximately $86 million. That was it. No fanfare, no hype, and no 30-minute special airing on live television for millions to watch. When he was asked if he wanted to experience what LeBron and Bosh did that summer, Durant said that he was happy in Oklahoma City and was glad that he would be staying for five more seasons. That loyalty added to the legend of his character and showed how he valued being part of the game.

Durant's popularity was soaring due to his clean image. However, it was only when US President Barack Obama wanted to play pick-up basketball with him at the White House that Durant realized how popular he was. Durant, with sneakers and a basketball in the trunk of his car, took teammates Eric Maynor and James Harden with him and played 5-on-5 basketball with the President of the United States of America.

The momentum from his USA Basketball experience and his date with the POTUS catapulted Kevin Durant into an elite class of players, though he was only 22 years old. He would use that momentum to his advantage and would lead try to lead the Thunder to greater heights in the new season. With his unparalleled talent in putting the ball through the hoop and in swishing in cold-hearted shots, Durant was not only becoming one of the most talented young stars, but was in a class reserved for the most elite. He was only entering his fourth season.

Durant started the new season with back-to-back identical 30-point games against the Chicago Bulls and the Detroit Pistons in wins for the OKC Thunder. Kevin Durant, throughout the early juncture of the year, would score at almost the same pace as when he won the scoring title just a season before. He was as consistent in putting the sphere through the basket as anybody else in the league. And with KD's penchant for scoring big baskets, the Thunder improved their pace from the previous season. They won 17 of their first 25 games.

One of Durant's best games early on in the season was on December 25, 2010, where he helped the Thunders give the Oklahoma City fans a 114-106 victory for the holidays. His numbers were quite impressive, not only for the 44 points in just under 41 minutes, but he also had seven rebounds (six on defense), four assists, two steals, and two blocks for a well-rounded game. But being the top scoring player in the match would be a common theme through most of the season.

Less than a month later, Durant made 40 points in the Thunder's 109-100 home win over the Memphis Grizzlies – a game where he also collected eight rebounds (seven on defense), four assists, and one block. Blocked shots have also become a common theme for Durant's season, and this season was another exhibit for that case since he had at least one block in 46 games. After that performance, KD had to encore when he scored at least 30 points in the next two games, which were both wins for the Thunder.

On January 26, 2011, Kevin Durant had one of the most memorable performances all season long. In an overtime battle that saw KD statistically fighting against the Minnesota Timberwolves' Kevin Love, the OKC forward tied his career high of 47 points while also grabbing 18 rebounds. Meanwhile, Love had 31 points and 21 rebounds in that battle of two young stars. Not done with his rampage, Kevin Durant had 40 points in his next game two days later in a win versus the Washington Wizards.

Kevin Durant, after back-to-back games of scoring at least 40 points then had 33 points and ten rebounds against the powerhouse Miami Heat team in a narrow loss. Nevertheless, he bounced back big to score 43 points and grab ten boards in a win versus the New Orleans Hornets in the next game. That was the third time he scored at least 40 points in a span of four games. He also had a streak of five consecutive double-double games in scoring and rebounding at the same moment.

A year after coming off the bench in the 2010 NBA All-Star Game, Durant would be a starter in the 2011 All-Star Game on February 20, 2011, at the Staples Center in Los Angeles, California. Playing with a starting lineup that included the Lakers' Kobe Bryant, New Orleans' Chris Paul, Denver's Carmelo Anthony, and San Antonio's Tim Duncan, Durant scored 34 points with three rebounds, two each of assists, steals, and blocks as the West defeated the East 148-143. In any other game, Durant would have probably been the player of the game, but the game's MVP Award went to Bryant, who had 37 points, 14 rebounds, and three steals.

After the All-Star break, Kevin Durant's performances were less than spectacular than what he spoiled the fans to getting used to. Nevertheless, he was playing within the flow of the game more and was getting his teammates involved more than ever as the OKC Thunder improved at that point of the season after trading away Jeff Green for the Celtics' Kendrick Perkins, a defensive center. Despite not putting on any more explosive performances while the Thunder were on a run for a good playoff spot, Kevin Durant's consistency had him scoring at least 20 points in all but three of the games he played to end the season.

Kevin Durant would hold on to his scoring title for one more season after averaging 27.7 points together with 6.8 rebounds and 2.7 assists that season. He was once again First Team All-NBA and was already arguably the most dangerous scorer the league has ever seen since Kobe Bryant was in his prime. Durant would also led the Thunder to another improved season. They were the fourth seed in the West and finished with 55 wins.

While Kevin Durant's steady performances were crucial in helping the OKC Thunder improve by leaps and bounds that season, it was ultimately a franchise effort that led to the rise of the youngsters in Oklahoma City. Durant was not the only improving star in OKC as the 2010-11 season also saw spitfire guard Russell Westbrook joining the All-Star squad for the first time in his career. With Westbrook rising to the level of an All-Star, Durant was not alone in carrying the offensive load of the Thunder and had a reliable secondary scorer that could also make plays for others.

The duo of Durant and Westbrook were indeed the key factor in the rise of the Thunder. Nevertheless, the other young pieces together with the veterans also made it possible for Oklahoma

City to improve by leaps and bounds. The trade to get Kendrick Perkins allowed the Thunder to put defensive specialist Serge Ibaka in the power forward spot to alleviate a lot of pressure from the other defenders on the team. With a frontline of Perkins and Ibaka, Durant and Westbrook could focus their might on offense.

On the bench, James Harden was also benefitted by the trade that sent Jeff Green to Boston. Green used to be the tertiary scorer for the Thunder, but was a defensive liability on the starting spot. With Green gone, Harden became the third option for Oklahoma City, and his numbers improved ever since that trade. Harden's bench production only served to make things easier for the Thunder starters.

With Kevin Durant backed up by several other young and talented players that had significant roles for the team, the Oklahoma City Thunder were going to be a terrifying team entering the 2011 postseason, especially because of their youthful legs and insatiable hunger to become an elite squad. Just a year after barely making the playoffs, the Thunder were legitimate contenders.

In his first playoff game that season, Kevin Durant was unstoppable from the field in their matchup against the Denver

Nuggets. He had a then-playoff career high 41 points on 13 out of 22 shooting from the field and 12 out of 15 from the foul line to beat the Nuggets and draw first blood in the series. It was a sign that Durant meant business in the postseason as early as that first game.

Game 2 was a total team effort for the Thunder, who went 2-0 with a convincing 17-point win in Oklahoma City. Durant had 23 points, and Westbrook and Harden both scored well to ease the pressure off the two-time scoring champion. And with Serge Ibaka playing like an All-Star in Game 3, Kevin Durant's 26 points on a difficult shooting night were more than enough to give the Thunder an insurmountable 3-0 lead in the series.

Despite the fact that Durant and Westbrook both scored at least 30 points in what was supposed to be a closeout bout in Game 4, the Nuggets still managed to extend the series by at least one more game to prevent a series sweep. But Kevin Durant would seal the Denver Nuggets' fate by scoring 41 points in Game 5, much like what he did in the opening bout. He made 14 of his 27 attempts from the floor in his second 40-point playoff game.

The Western Conference playoff picture was wide open due to the upset win of the eighth-seeded Memphis Grizzlies over the top-seeded San Antonio Spurs, and due to the skid that the two-time defending champions Los Angeles Lakers were experiencing. If there were a right time for the Thunder to make some noise as a young and upstart team, it would be in that year's postseason.

In the second round, the Thunder would face the defensively-tough Memphis Grizzlies. Riding the momentum that they used to beat the Spurs in the first round, the Grizzlies would defeat the Thunder in Game 1 despite Durant's 33-point effort. Banking on their trio of young scorers' combined 71-point output, OKC would tie the series at one win apiece. Durant had 26, Westbrook scored 24, and Harden dropped 21 off the bench.

A fourth quarter outburst from the Memphis Grizzlies forced an overtime period for Game 3. The OKC Thunder were unable to weather the storm in the extra period as Memphis survived the double-double efforts of Kevin Durant and Russell Westbrook. That overtime game would not be the highlight of the series, but the pivotal fourth game was an instant classic.

With neither team able to get separation from the other, Game 4 went into three extra overtime periods. It was Memphis that forced all of the three overtime periods. Nevertheless, Kevin Durant was the deciding force that gave the victory to the Oklahoma City Thunder, who tied the series 2-2. Durant scored six points in the third overtime period despite the tired legs that were already playing nearly 57 points. KD finished with 35 points and 13 rebounds while his running mate finished with 40.

Riding on the momentum of a triple-overtime win, the younger and fresher legs of the OKC Thunder were able to run through the Grizzlies in Game 5 to take the series lead. In only 30 minutes of action, KD scored 19 points as the bench did most of the damage in that blowout win. However, he would be limited to his worst playoff performance in Game 6 when the Grizzlies managed to force a deciding seventh game. Durant shot 3 out of 14 for only 11 points in that loss.

In the most important Game 7 of his young career, Kevin Durant proved that he was a clutch performer when he torched the Grizzlies for 39 points on 13 out of 25 shooting from the field. In addition to Durant's clutch shooting performance in that game, his partner Westbrook put up a Game 7 triple-double to join an elite class of clutch performers who have also done the same. The win would push the Thunder to their first Conference Finals appearance since relocating to Oklahoma City just a year after they made they reached the playoffs for the first time.

Kevin Durant opened the series by scoring 40 points on the hungry and streaking Dallas Mavericks led by a focused and unstoppable Dirk Nowitzki, one of the players KD was compared to when he first came into the league. He made 55% of his attempts and 18 of his 19 attempts from the foul stripe. However, he was overshadowed by the 48 points of Dirk, who seemed to torch everyone the Thunder put on him. With his length, adept shooting touch, and patented unblockable one-legged fadeaway, Nowitzki displayed first hand to Durant what it was to become an unstoppable scorer in that win for Dallas.

After losing Game 1, the Thunder would win Game 2 thanks to the all-around efforts of all of their young pieces. The bench was also equally productive in their first playoff win in the Conference Finals. However, that was their lone win versus the Mavs as Dallas completely schooled the Thunder with their combination of offensive hunger and defensive mastery.

Throughout the next three games of the Conference Finals, Kevin Durant was unable to shake loose the defensive strategy that the Mavs put on him. From Shawn Marion to DeShawn Stevenson and even the smaller Jason Kidd, Durant saw different defensive looks that prevented him from exploding for huge scoring outputs. After dropping 40 in Game 1, he was limited to an average of 25 points on 40% shooting in the next four games. The Dallas Mavericks would beat them in five games and eventually win the NBA crown in the Finals over the Miami Heat.

Trip to the NBA Finals, Breaking the Trio

After breaking through to the Western Conference Finals in his fourth year and only his second appearance in the playoffs, Kevin Durant could only lead the OKC Thunder to greater heights in the upcoming seasons. The team and their key players were rising quicker than any other in the history of the league. Even the sky was not the limit for the streaking Oklahoma City Thunder and their superstar Kevin Durant.

However, the Thunder's chance to further develop into a powerhouse was put on hold as the NBA went into a labor dispute that forced a lockout pending resolution of any issues that the union had with the owners. The lockout prevented teams from using facilities and practicing together. Some players grew stagnant, and others got out of shape. But not Kevin Durant.

Ever the obsessed basketball enthusiast, Kevin Durant did what he could as an individual to further hone his skills and improve his conditioning. He started off by playing in several exhibition games and amateur tournaments. He made appearances in Asian countries such as China and even the Philippines. He went to play in the Drew League and even put on a show in Oklahoma City in an exhibition game that featured friends Chris Paul, Blake Griffin, Carmelo Anthony, and James Harden, among others.[vi]

The level of Kevin Durant's activity over the long offseason together with his trips and his other basketball-related events only made the Oklahoma City Thunder superstar an even more famous player. His loyalty to his city and organization, dedication to the game, and his ever-growing hunger to become elite and succeed in the world of basketball had people billing him as the anti-LeBron James.[vii]

In contrast to LeBron James' "Decision" in 2010, Kevin Durant stayed in OKC by signing a max contract. While James was off to Miami in search of rings with an already established All-Star crew, Durant would try to develop his team of future stars by leading a young and talented Oklahoma City Thunder squad. While "The King" was nowhere to be sighted in popular events in the offseason because he was working to regain the trust of the fans that scorned him, KD was out there earning the praises of basketball junkies worldwide to become one of the most popular talents in the NBA. And while LeBron loved the bright lights and party scene of Miami, Kevin was in the blue-collar city of Oklahoma working his tail off to become a better superstar.

As early as then, Kevin Durant was already getting billed as the rival and usurper to LeBron James' throne as the best small forward and basketball player in the world. The contrast in styles were all too many between the two superstars as Durant, and in no time, he was regarded as the number two player in the league behind only James himself.

As the league has consistently triumphed and earned in marketing big name rivals over the years, Durant versus James was one that had the potential to join the ranks of Russell versus Chamberlain, Magic versus Bird, Jordan versus Thomas, and Kobe versus LeBron. It was a rising star trying to become great in a small market team that was building through the draft against the established alpha male that joined a group of equally talented alphas to try and win NBA titles.

But even if the media was trying to portray Kevin Durant and LeBron James as rivals, there was no personal animosity or tension between the two elite players. In fact, KD and LBJ were friends. During the extended lockout period, Durant and James even worked out together in the latter's hometown of Akron, Ohio. The workouts involved strength training and basketball-related activities meant to improve their respective skills.[viii] No matter how much the media would like to bill them bitter opposites to one another, the two stars left the rivalry on the court.

All the basketball activity and offseason workout sessions individually or with other great players only served to make Kevin Durant a much better player in preparation for an upcoming deep run for him and his team during the 2011-12 season. But Durant was not the only improved player in OKC. Russell Westbrook reprised his role as the secondary All-Star while James Harden, in what would become his final year with the Thunder, rose to become the most elite backup.

When the season started late in December, Kevin Durant immediately went to work, scoring at least 30 points in the first four games of the Thunder, who went 5-0. Had Durant played the full length of their fifth game, which was an easy win against the Phoenix Suns, he would have started the season scoring 30 or more points in each of their first five wins.

The run that Durant and the Thunder experienced at the early part of the season would not slow down. The best scorer in the entire NBA was not merely scoring in bunches, but was also rebounding at a rate higher than he ever had before. Kevin

Durant scored at least 20 points in all but 18 of his first 20 games. He even had seven double-double performances.

Late in January up until early February of 2012, Kevin Durant would record five consecutive double-double performances. It all started with his 37-point, 14-rebound game in a win versus the Golden State Warriors on January 27. Durant's consistency had the Oklahoma City Thunder winning 20 of their first 25 games. Durant had already scored at least 30 points in 10 of those outings.

Right when Kevin Durant was about to enter his third All-Star Game, he solidified his name as one of the brightest stars in the league by dropping 51 big points on the Denver Nuggets in a win on February 19. And while most of Durant's high-scoring games featured tons of attempts from the free throw line, KD would only score 8 points from the foul stripe as he swished in 19 of his 28 field goal attempts in that game to further prove that he was the most lethal scorer of his generation. With Westbrook scoring 40 in that game, Durant and his point guard became only the 10th duo in NBA history to score at least 40 points each in one game. Not feeling any fatigue the very next day, he scored 31 on the Hornets.

During the midseason classic, Kevin Durant would score 36 points in the All-Star game and was named the All-Star Game's Most Valuable Player. Durant was indeed the brightest star that shone that night even as he scored just as many points as his rival LeBron James. On a side note, the spotlight was stolen by his idol Kobe Bryant who clinched the All-Star scoring record by scoring 27 points. Running mate Russell Westbrook also did well by scoring 21 off the bench.

Nearly a month after the All-Star Game, Kevin Durant had another one of the best games of the season. In a fantastic win against the Minnesota Timberwolves, Durant and his team force two overtime periods while surviving a career night from Kevin Love. Durant scored 40 points and grabbed 17 rebounds. Meanwhile, Westbrook scored 45 points. With those performances, KD and Russ became the only duo in NBA history to score at least 40 points each in one game twice, and it happened in the same season.

Kevin Durant would have two more 40-point games that season. The next one was on April 6 in a loss to the Indiana Pacers, and the last one was against the Minnesota Timberwolves again. His 43 points were enough to beat the Wolves, who were missing the services of Love. Durant would then score at least 30 points in the final three games of the season to hold on to his narrow lead in points per game over Kobe Bryant's resilient season.

Kevin Durant would win his third consecutive scoring title to become the only player since Michael Jordan to win it three straight seasons. He averaged 28 points, eight rebounds, 3.5 assists, and 1.3 steals. His field goal percentage also jumped to 49.6%. Durant would lead the Thunder to a record of 47-19 to win the second seed in the Western Conference. Because of the performances that Kevin Durant was putting up every night together with his consistency in helping the Thunder improve each year, he was nearly voted the NBA's Most Valuable Player. He finished a close second to LeBron James in that regard. The MVP race only served to grow the rivalry between Durant and James.

Kevin Durant would open the postseason run with a 25-point performance in a narrow win over the Dallas Mavericks, the very same team that had dominated them in the previous Conference Finals. With the Mavs being a very different team from the one that had won the title just a year ago, the Thunder would use their youthful legs to beat them three more times to sweep them from the postseason. Durant had two double-double performances in the series after barely even needing to score in bunches.

Just a season after losing to Dirk Nowitzki's Dallas Mavericks, Kevin Durant defeated his tormentor from a year before in a convincing fashion in the opening round. More importantly, they were the one to dethrone the defending champions and were quickly becoming a favorite for the title. And for Kevin Durant's part, he had learned a thing or two from his battles with Dirk. He learned to become unguardable. From time to time, KD would use Nowitzki's patented one-legged fadeaway to get more separation and space from the defender. He learned how to use his height and length more often to become virtually unstoppable. This was a Kevin Durant with a quickly maturing game. He was becoming even more dangerous than he already was.

In the second round, the Thunder would meet the Los Angeles Lakers led by Kobe Bryant. While the Lakers were much more experienced than the boys from OKC, the Thunder were younger and hungrier than their older counterparts. This led to a 29-point Game 1 victory for Oklahoma City, who put their fresher and younger legs to good use.

Clamped down by the defensive capabilities of the Lakers in Game 2, Kevin Durant would struggle from the field in a low-scoring output. Nevertheless, his 22 points were still enough to seal the deal for the Thunder, who were now up 2-0 in the series.

The OKC Thunder had won six straight games in the playoffs and were yet to be defeated.

In a shootout between Kevin Durant and Kobe Bryant, the Lakers managed to beat the Thunder for their lone win in the series as they banked on the 36 points of their all-time great superstar. Meanwhile, Durant scored 31 points despite the loss. However, Game 4 was a total effort by the Thunder duo to survive the 38 points of Bryant. Kevin Durant finished with 31 points and 13 rebounds while Westbrook exploded for 37 points as he made minced meat out of the Lakers' backcourt defense. And despite the 42 points from the Black Mamba, the Thunder closed the series out thanks to another combined effort from KD and Russ.

Facing the ever-dominant and consistent San Antonio Spurs was not an easy task for the still young and inexperienced Oklahoma City Thunder. The inexperience was quite evident when they melted down in the fourth quarter of their Game 1 bout to lose to the Spurs, who were title favorites that season. And despite the 31 points of Durant in Game 2, the Spurs raced to a 2-0 lead and were slated to sweep the series once again after going 10-0 in the playoffs.

In OKC, Durant and company combined to beat their heavily-favored opponents on the defensive end. Despite only 22 points from KD, it was enough for the Thunder to snap the 10-game winning streak of the Spurs. With Kevin Durant scoring 31 points and putting up eight assists in Game 4 while being backed by a perfect 11-11 game from Serge Ibaka, the Thunder would tie the series 2-2 and make the Western Conference Finals a battle.

Game 5 was the pivotal bout of that series given that whoever won it would gain control of the series and would possibly make the NBA Finals. Proving once again that he was a clutch and efficient performer, Durant scored 27 points on 10 out of 19 shooting from the field to help defeat the Spurs and get a 3-2 series lead over them after starting the series 0-2.

In what was a display of stamina, conditioning, and mental toughness for Kevin Durant in Game 6, the Thunder would put the San Antonio Spurs away in six games to reach the NBA Finals for the first time since relocating to Oklahoma City. It was also the first time since Gary Payton led the Seattle SuperSonics against Michael Jordan's Chicago Bulls back in the 90's. Durant played all 48 minutes in that closeout game and had 34 points, 14 rebounds, and five assists in one of his better performances that offseason.

By defeating the Spurs in the Conference Finals, the Oklahoma City Thunder have completed their quest for Western supremacy. They have become to heirs to the throne of the Western powerhouses after beating the three best teams the conference has seen since 1999. Since that year, the Spurs (4 titles), the Lakers (5 titles), and the Mavericks (1 title) have all been the Finalists for the Western Conference and have won 10 of the last 13 NBA championships. By defeating those three powerhouse teams, the Thunder unofficially ushered in a changing of the guard in the Western Conference.

Because Oklahoma City were on their way to face the Miami Heat in the 2012 NBA Finals, it was going to be a battle of two teams with several stars. The Thunder were banking on their trio of Kevin Durant, Russell Westbrook, and Sixth Man of the Year James Harden. Meanwhile, the Heat had their own Big Three of LeBron James, Dwyane Wade, and Chris Bosh. However, the main narrative was the matchup between KD and LBJ. The two best players in the world were finally meeting on the grandest stage of basketball to battle for their first NBA championship.

The championship round started, and Thunder took the first game of the NBA Finals at home on June 12, 2012, in a 105-94 victory in front of a sold-out Chesapeake Energy Arena in

Oklahoma City. The momentum was building for a city that had not had any professional sports franchises, let alone one that was competing for a main event league championship.

Durant led the way with 36 points with a rate of 60 percent shooting from the field, going 12 for 20. Beyond the three-point arc, he made half of his shots (4 of 8) and an additional eight out of nine from the free throw line. The rest of his statistics line included eight rebounds, four assists, and one blocked shot. His teammate Russell Westbrook was the second part of the one-two punch with 27 points, eight rebounds, 11 assists, and one steal.

The excitement grew as the discussions that Miami's Big Three, possibly being overrated, were the next biggest group since Boston's trio of stars that won a championship in 2008 with Kevin Garnett, Ray Allen, and Paul Pierce. LeBron James and the Heat, who were denied by the Dallas Mavericks of the title last season, did not go away.

The momentum died quickly in the second game as Miami defeated the Thunder 100-96 on June 14, 2012. Durant had 32 points, but only collected three rebounds and one assist–a significant drop from the Game 1 victory, and it was not enough to keep up with LeBron James scoring 32 points, Dwayne Wade's 24, and Chris Bosh's 15 rebounds and 16 points.

Durant's numbers dropped again with only 25 points in the Game 3 loss on June 17, 2012, a 91-85 loss in Miami. The Heat's star player, James, was starting to pick up steam as he scored 29 points and had 14 rebounds for a double-double. The Heat won Game 4 on June 19, 2012, with a score of 104-98. Durant had 28 points in the only pretty-looking statistic on the sheet. Westbrook was the brighter star with 43 points, seven rebounds, and five assists, but the other six Thunder players failed to reach double-digit scoring. James Harden was third with eight points and ten rebounds, shooting a dismal 20 percent from the field.

There was hope in Oklahoma City that if the Thunder could bring the series back to the Chesapeake Energy Center, they could turn it around from 3-1 down. However, the Heat took care of business defeating Oklahoma City 121-106 in Game 5 to clinch the NBA Championship.

Durant was able to play one of his best playoff games individually with 32 points and 11 rebounds. He also had a couple of steals and a blocked shot. Westbrook and Harden had 19 points of their own while Derek Fisher had 11 points. But

Miami had their star players step up in a series-clinching scenario as four players scored 20 or more points. James had 26 points with 11 rebounds and 13 assists in a triple-double to help him win his first NBA Championship. Chris Bosh had 24 points, Mike Miller had 23, and Dwayne Wade had 20. It is also worth noting that Shane Battier (11) and Mario Chalmers (10) both reached double digits on the scoreboard.

In the end, Miami blasted through the OKC defense to win the next four games and win their first title in the Big Three era. LeBron James gained the lead in his rivalry with Kevin Durant, while the latter was forced to see the better all-around player hoisting his first NBA trophy. The Thunder would go back to the drawing board, disappointed that they had lost in the finals but confident that they could win it all the following season.

Despite the deep run that the Oklahoma City Thunder experienced under the leadership and transcendent skills of Kevin Durant, there were growing concerns among critics nonetheless. What was perceived as a concern and problem for those outside the franchise circle was the pecking order in the Oklahoma City Thunder locker room. While there were no major rifts between Kevin Durant and Russell Westbrook, nobody was sure who the alpha between the two should be.

It was a given that Kevin Durant had the bigger shot share during the regular season. However, the number of shots he was taking were not significantly more than what Westbrook was shooting. Both players were attempting at least 19 shots per game, but Durant was obviously the more efficient scorer given that he was averaging nearly five more points. Though the number of shots that Russ was taking was a growing concern in the regular season since he was the less efficient shooter, there were hardly any problems as far as the Thunder were concerned because they were still winning.

The postseason was a different story, however. In the playoffs, Russell Westbrook was taking more shots than Kevin Durant. KD was shooting 19.2 attempts per game while making an efficient 51.7%. On the other hand, Russ was putting up 20.4 shots but was only making a little over 43% of them. Given those numbers, there was no doubt that Durant was the more efficient shooter and better scorer. It also meant that Westbrook probably had no business taking more shots than the three-time scoring champion.

The major critique was that Kevin Durant would have scored more if Westbrook had focused on passing the ball and shooting shots he knew he could make. The Thunder may have even been a better team had KD been allowed to dominate the ball more.

Nevertheless, neither of the two players had any ego problems that derailed the chemistry of the Thunder, unlike how Shaquille O'Neal and Kobe Bryant could not coexist back in the day. Durant and Westbrook adored and mutually respected one another's personalities and abilities.

Without James Harden, 50-40-90 Season

While the Oklahoma City Thunder enjoined an NBA Finals appearance largely because of Kevin Durant, the superstar forward could not have done it all alone. Of course there was Russell Westbrook, who was one of the fastest rising point guards in the NBA. The third head of the offensive trio was James Harden, who had just won the Sixth Man of the Year award. With three supreme talents from the perimeter, one could only imagine how far the Thunder could get.

As much as they would have wanted to keep their core offensive trio, the Thunder were financially hampered. Over the past two seasons, they signed both Kevin Durant and Russell Westbrook to max contracts. And with James Harden demanding to get paid big while Serge Ibaka was also equally deserving of a good contract, the OKC Thunder franchise had to choose between their best scorer off the bench or their best shot blocker. Thinking that Ibaka was a better complement to Durant and Westbrook, the front office shipped Harden over to Houston in exchange for the Rockets' Kevin Martin. While Martin was a reliable scorer, he was not James Harden.

Despite the loss of their third best scorer, the OKC Thunder still had Kevin Durant leading the charge. He would have to fill in for the scoring and playmaking duties left by the versatile Harden. And while the Thunder were projected to suffer a minor decrease in production without The Bearded One, they would show that the following season would be their best yet.

Kevin Durant would start the 2012-13 season with three consecutive double-double outputs though his scoring was not in the range everyone was accustomed to. His lack of offensive production also had the Thunder losing two of their first three games. In fact, it would even take KD a while before he went back to the scoring champion mode he had been in the past three seasons.

Durant's first performance scoring above 30 points was his ninth game of the season. In that loss to the Grizzlies, he had 34 points, ten rebounds, and five assists. Four days later on November 18, 2012, KD had his first career triple-double when he recorded 25 points, 13 rebounds, and ten assists in a win over the Golden State Warriors just when the Thunder started streaking.

Starting off what was going to be a 12-game winning streak for OKC, Kevin Durant would have 37 points in an overtime affair versus the Philadelphia 76ers. He would have seven games scoring above 30 points in that winning streak before capping it all off by dropping 41 points and 13 rebounds on the Atlanta Hawks. After that win, the Thunder were 21-4 during the first 25 games of the season.

After a rough start concerning scoring the basketball, Kevin Durant's point production normalized as the season progressed. After dropping 41 on the Hawks on December 19, he had 40 against the Dallas Mavericks on December 27 just two days after losing their Finals rematch against the Miami Heat. He would then have 42 points on January 11, 2013, against the Lakers before scoring 41 in a win over the Phoenix Suns three days later. The two 40-point games sandwiched his 33 points against the Portland Trailblazers. At that point of the season, the Thunder were the Western Conference leaders.

As a testament to his scoring greatness, Kevin Durant would score 52 points just four days after scoring 41 over the Suns. In that January 18 game, he made 13 of his 31 attempts and did most of his damage from the free-throw line by draining all of his 21 attempts. That performance sealed the overtime win for the Thunder, who had already mastered the Mavericks at that point. Durant would not slow down as he scored at least 30 points in the next three games.

Right before the All-Star break, Durant would score 40 again. However, despite his best efforts, he was still unable to best LeBron James' Miami Heat in their second meeting of the season despite putting up a better scoring performance against The King, who had 39 in that head-to-head matchup between the two best players of that era.

In his fourth All-Star Game, Kevin Durant was once again a starter for the Western Conference. He was the third leading vote-getter behind only Kobe Bryant and LeBron James in that regard. Durant would also lead the Western Conference in scoring en route to another win for his team. However, it was Chris Paul who would go home with the All-Star MVP trophy after his 20-point 15-assist output.

Though it would come at a loss to James Harden's new team, Kevin Durant would have his second career triple-double against the Houston Rockets in his first game after the All-Star break. He had 16 points, 12 rebounds, and 11 assists.

What made Kevin Durant a unique superstar was not only his unreal scoring virtuosity, but also his receptiveness when it came to improving his game by observing and losing to other great players. One case in point was when he lost to Dirk Nowitzki back in the 2011 Western Conference Finals, but came back the following season learning how to become unguardable like the German power forward. And after losing to LeBron James in the 2012 Finals, Durant went into the 2012-13 season trying to be a better all-around player by passing the ball better.

Another instance of his display of his much-improved passing skills was when he recorded his third triple-double just a week after his second. In that demolition job against the New Orleans Hornets, KD quickly piled the stats up as he only played 27 minutes but finished with 18 points, 11 rebounds, and ten assists. Like LeBron, he was trying to get his teammates involved by making sure they were also contributing points.

Under the leadership of Kevin Durant, the Thunder would breeze through their final 29 games after the All-Star break by winning 21 of those outings. Durant did not even need to play in the final game of the season. The OKC Thunder had already clinched the best record in the conference. They would finish the season with a Western Conference high of 60 wins as against 22 losses. Durant averaged 28.1 points, 7.9 rebounds, and a then career-best 4.6 assists.

With the way he was playing, KD was once again a strong candidate for the MVP award only to lose it to LeBron James for the second season in a row. Nevertheless, Kevin Durant was once again phenomenal, although this time he failed to defend his scoring title and lost it via close margin to Carmelo Anthony of the New York Knicks. Durant became the youngest member of the 50-40-90 club, an elite group of NBA stars led by legendary Larry Bird, Mark Price, Reggie Miller, Steve Nash, and Dirk Nowitzki. This group shot at least 50 percent from the field, 40 percent from three point area, and 90 percent from the foul line during an NBA season.

The Thunder were looking like title favorites early in the playoffs before Russell Westbrook was injured during their first round series against the Houston Rockets. Durant and the Thunder struggled without Westbrook. Oklahoma City was up 3-0 in the first round series after Durant scored 41 points and 14 rebounds in the Thunder's 104-101 win at Houston on April 27, 2013.

But the absence of Westbrook would be tough on the Thunder for the next two games – a Game 3 loss 105-103 on April 29,

2013, and a 107-100 defeat on May 1, 2013. Durant still played well in both games with 38 points and eight rebounds in the Game 4 loss on the road. The return to Oklahoma City did not bring immediate success to the team, even though Durant had 36 points, seven rebounds, and seven assists against the Rockets.

While Durant is considered the top star for Oklahoma City, it is always great when someone jumps up from the bench when another star player is out with an injury. Oklahoma City won Game 6 against the Houston Rockets on the road 103-94 on May 3, 2012. This is due not only to Durant's 27 points, eight rebounds, and six assists, but also Kevin Martin's 25 points in nearly 40 minutes of time after Kendrick Perkins was injured.

Martin scored another 25 points off of the bench in the Thunder's first game against the Memphis Grizzlies in the Western Conference semifinals – a 93-91 win on May 5, 2013. Durant led all players with 35 points, 15 defensive rebounds, and six assists. His performance was highlighted by a 19-foot jumper to give the Thunder the 91-90 lead that was extended by a couple of free throws from Reggie Jackson.

But the Grizzlies had a more complete and healthy team compared to the injury-riddled Thunder and would win the next four games to advance to the Western Conference finals. The playoff exit was no fault of Durant's. He scored double-doubles in Games 2 and 3 (36 and 25 points, respectively) with 11 rebounds in each. He also scored 27 and 21 points in the fourth and fifth games, but Oklahoma City would then watch the rest of the playoffs from home – with Miami winning a second-straight NBA Championships over the San Antonio Spurs.

After seeing LeBron James hoisting his second championship trophy, the competitor in Kevin Durant finally snapped. He was tired of being the bridesmaid. He was always watching people come first before him. In the 2007 NBA Draft, he came second after Greg Oden was chosen first. For two straight seasons, he finished second to LeBron in the MVP voting. In 2012, he and his team finished second to the Miami Heat for the title. And for the past three seasons, he was regarded as only the second best player in the NBA.[ix]

While he did not explicitly say it, Durant was also second in other aspects in that recently concluded season. He finished a close second to Carmelo Anthony for the league scoring title, which would have been KD's fourth consecutive one. He would even finish second on his team in shot attempts as Russell Westbrook, ever regarded as a ball hog, was putting up more shots than he was despite being far less efficient.

For three seasons, it had been difficult for Durant to be second in a lot of aspects when he was trying his best to be on top. Had he played in another generation, KD could have been the best player in the NBA. But he had to concede to the fact that he had to contend with LeBron James, who he still treated as a good friend. Nevertheless, Durant was never so tired of finishing second in his life. For once in his life, he wanted to be regarded as the best.[ix] That would be his mindset as he geared himself up for the following season.

MVP Season

Heading into the new season, the OKC Thunder were troubled by the news that their All-Star point guard still was not in his top health after the offseason surgery he had to undergo. The bigger problem was that they were wondering if Russell Westbrook would even return to his explosive self after seeing as how Derrick Rose was hampered and degraded by a similar injury. With those problems in the back of their minds, the front office was wondering how far they could get with only Kevin Durant shouldering the load.

Despite his slender build, Durant was ready to carry the burdens of a hopeful Oklahoma City Thunder even though their point guard was not a hundred percent. Though Westbrook would play 25 games early in the season, it was clear that he was struggling with the injury he had just suffered a few months before. He would again be shut down late in December and would not return until February. In the times when Russ was struggling and absent, it was a Kevin Durant show for the Thunder.

Durant immediately made it known to the world that he was not about to finish second once again that season. In his first game, which was a win against the Utah Jazz, KD more than made up for the absence of his running mate as he exploded for 42 points, which included 22 from the free throw line. Over the course of the next nine games, he would score at least 30 points in five of those outings.

On December 1, 2013, Kevin Durant would record his first triple-double of the season in a win over the Minnesota Timberwolves by putting up 32 points, ten rebounds, and 12 assists. That win was also the seventh straight for the Thunder, who would win as many as eight at that early juncture. And when the streak ended, they would win another nine straight games in December despite the struggles of Russell Westbrook. Because their other All-Star player was not in his best form, KD was the key component for the Thunder, who went 22-4 in their first 26 games.

The moment that Westbrook was finally shut down for a few months, Kevin Durant put on an offensive show of a lifetime. After ending 2013 with 37 points and 14 rebounds in a loss to the Trailblazers, he began 2014 by scoring 48 big points on the Timberwolves. He made 16 of his 32 field goal attempts in that game. Three days later, he would score 48 again in a loss to the Jazz.

After that second 48-point game, Kevin Durant would become an unstoppable scoring force for the Thunder. He would have 12 straight games of scoring at least 30 points. With those performances, he became only the 10th player in league history to score 30 or more points in at least ten consecutive games. It was also during that moment when he put on together a personal best of 41 straight games of scoring at least 25 points.

Kevin Durant was not short of highlight performances during that incredible run. On January 17, 2014, in a win over the Golden State Warriors, Durant scored a new career high of 54 points by draining 19 of his 28 shots and 11 of his 13 free throw attempts. Four days later, he torched the Portland Trailblazers for 46 points in another win for the Thunder.

Despite putting up terrific scoring numbers, Durant never forgot about getting his teammates involved in the offense. He would have 32 points, 14 rebounds, and ten assists on January 25 in a win over the Philadelphia 76ers. In the very next game, he dropped 41 on the Atlanta Hawks. Durant would end his 12-game streak of scoring at least 30 points when he had 26 points in only 30 minutes in a blowout win over the Brooklyn Nets. He could have extended the streak had he chosen to play longer. That win was also the Thunder's tenth consecutive in Durant's scoring tear.

On February 9, Durant nearly had his first 40-point triple-double after piling up 41 points, ten rebounds, and nine assists in a win over the New York Knicks. Four days after that, he had a similar stat line in a win against the Los Angeles Lakers when he recorded 43 points, 12 rebounds, and seven assists. That was all the momentum that Durant needed as he was on his way to his fifth All-Star Game.

Though Kevin Durant would fail to win the All-Star MVP after scoring 38 points in a loss to the Eastern Conference Finals, he was finding himself in a familiar conversation—the MVP race. Kevin Durant was always a key name in the MVP conversation, though he would finish second in two straight seasons. However, during the 2013-14 season, nobody would deny the fact that Durant was the leading candidate for that award even though

LeBron James was still putting up great numbers in another fantastic season.

With Kevin Durant putting up fantastic numbers all season long, not just in scoring but the other aspects of the game, the conversation of who between him and LeBron James was the better player only grew hotter. Durant's season was closing the gap between himself and James. It may have even catapulted KD to the position as the best player in the world despite the fact that LeBron was still just as transcendent as he has ever been. The reason Durant was leading in the MVP race was not because LeBron's production had fallen off. It was simply because KD had surpassed him in productivity and impact that season.

The same impact and productivity were never more evident as Durant continued to torch the whole league after the All-Star break, even when Russell Westbrook returned to the lineup in full health. In another unreal performance from the soon-to-be four-time scoring champion, Kevin Durant would score 42 points in just 30 minutes of action in a 33-point win over the Sixers on March 4. Five days later, he had his third triple-double of the season after putting up 27 points, ten rebounds, and 12 assists in a loss to the Lakers. He quickly bounced back to drop 42 on the hapless Rockets.

In what was considered his best performance of the season, the leading MVP candidate would go into Toronto to break the hearts of Raptors fans. With the game going to two overtime periods, Durant hit the game-winner with only 1.7 seconds left to go to score a total of 51 points together with 12 rebounds and seven assists in what was a defining MVP performance for him.

Durant would end the season scoring at least 40 points two more times. Unfortunately, his streak of scoring at least 25 points would end versus the Sacramento Kings when he scored 23 points in 31 minutes. His streak ended at 41 as he broke Michael Jordan's record of 40. Had he chosen to extend it, he could have done it by demanding he be put on the floor longer to score one more basket. But Durant was not that type of player. Wins mattered more to him than personal accomplishments. He ended the season scoring 42 points over the Detroit Pistons.

With a total of 2,593 points through 81 games, Durant averaged a little more than 32 points per game for his fourth NBA scoring title in 2014. He was beaten by New York's Carmelo Anthony in 2013 after Durant won three straight titles from 2010 to 2012. With his fourth scoring title, Durant joined Chamberlain, Gervin, and Jordan as the only four players in league history to lead the NBA in scoring in four different seasons. Arguably the best statistical season he has ever had in his career, Durant also averaged 7.4 rebounds and a career-high 5.5 assists. He was not only scoring crazy throughout the season, but was also making sure he was getting his teammates involved.

Durant was putting up crazy all-around numbers all season long, and he led the Oklahoma City Thunder to a 59-23 record, which was only second to the San Antonio Spurs in the NBA. There was almost no arguing that he was going to be named the Most Valuable Player in the NBA.

Kevin Durant would be voted as the 2014 NBA MVP in the middle of the playoffs. Though the media would portray it as supposedly a close battle between him and LeBron James, there was no denying that KD would not finish second that season. He even won it by a wide margin, earning 119 out of 125 first place votes.

In one of the most memorable MVP speeches, Kevin Durant received the award in the most humble way possible. He never attributed the honor to his hard work and dedication, but took the time instead to individually thank everyone in the organization for how they contributed to his growth and development as a player. He spared nobody. Even Caron Butler, who the team had just acquired a few months prior, was part of that speech. Among all of his teammates, he thanked Russell Westbrook last.

Saving the best teammate for last, KD dismissed any notion about a rift between him and Russ and even thanked and encouraged his All-Star teammate to remain true to himself and never change his style for anybody. He said that he would be the first person to back Westbrook up whenever critics and detractors get too hard on him. Lastly, he would say that Russell Westbrook was equally deserving of the MVP award because his skills and dedication were on par, if not better, than Durant's.[x]

In one of the most iconic moments in MVP speech history, Kevin Durant would thank his mom last among all of the people that made an impact on his life. Durant would recount how his mom tried her best to give food and shelter to her two sons, even as a single mother. He could not thank her any more than calling her "the real MVP" as all the other people in the room stood up in unison to give a standing ovation to the woman that raised one of the best NBA players in league history.[x]

After ranting in the offseason about how he was always finishing second, Kevin Durant was now on top of the NBA landscape as arguably the best player that year. There was no questioning or doubting his place as one of the best, if not the best, athletes in that generation of basketball. He took the MVP and the mantle by force from LeBron James, who was still putting up crazy numbers. With a player efficiency rating of 29.8, there was no wondering how genuinely good Kevin Durant was that season. But the battle was not over. He may not have finished second in the MVP, but he still had to lead his team to a first place finish in the playoffs to become one of the all-time greats in the history of the league.

Despite being the better team throughout the season, the Oklahoma City Thunder would find it difficult to beat the Memphis Grizzlies in the first round of the playoffs even though both Durant and Westbrook were in full health. After winning Game 1, they would lose two straight to the Grizzlies, who went up 2-1 entering Game 4. But it was not because of a lack of effort on the part of KD, who averaged more than 30 points in those three games.

Defended firmly and tightly in Game 4, Durant shot only 5 out of 21 for 15 points as his Thunder fought another close bout against the Grizzlies. However, an unlikely hero in the form of backup point guard Reggie Jackson saved the series for the Thunder by scoring 32 points off the bench. The win would tie the series 2-2 and give them momentum to win two of the next three games. In those two wins to end the series, Kevin Durant combined for 69 points as the league MVP proved that he was indeed deserving of that award.

In the second round against the Los Angeles Clippers, Durant averaged 33.1 points and 9.3 rebounds per game during a series. The Thunder won in six games, even after a rough 122-105 loss in Game 1 at home. Durant would bounce back with a near triple-double in a 112-101 Game 2 victory on May 7, 2014, where Durant had 32 points, 12 rebounds, and nine assists. The Thunder would take Game 3 in Los Angeles with another 36 points from Durant, but the Clippers would bounce back in Game 4 to tie the series despite Durant scoring 40 points to lead all players.

In the fifth game, Durant would be a key player in the fifth game, which was a win for Oklahoma City 105-104 on May 13, 2014. Durant made a 27-foot three-pointer with 44 seconds left, and then another lay-up to bring the game within two. Teammate Westbrook had the ball behind the arc with six seconds left when he was followed by Clippers' Chris Paul. Westbrook would make all three to put them ahead for the win.

That momentum carried over to the Game 6 win as Durant scored 39 points and 16 rebounds, all on defense, for Oklahoma

City's 104-98 win to punch their ticket to the conference finals round. However, just as the Western Conference Finals began, injury struck the Thunder once again.

Big man Serge Ibaka missed the first two games of the Western Conference Finals, enabling the San Antonio Spurs to take a 2-0 lead. This was highlighted by the Spurs 112-77 win in Game 2 on May 21, 2014, in a game where Westbrook and Durant only scored 15 points each – which they would not relinquish. The Thunder battled back to a 2-2 tie thanks in part to Westbrook's 26 points and Durant's 25 in Game 3 on May 25, 2014. A couple of days later, the Thunder won Game 4 behind the one-two punch of Westbrook (41) and Durant (30) to lead the way.

But with veterans like Tim Duncan, Tony Parker, and Manu Ginobili, the Spurs knew how to create and maintain the drive to get to the NBA Finals. Despite the tied series, the Spurs had gained too much momentum ran away with the next two games to beat the Thunder and eventually win the 2014 NBA Championship.

The Western Conference Finals loss to the San Antonio Spurs were not because of a lack of effort on Durant or any of his other teammates. The Spurs, at that point of the season, were just too good for anyone to beat them. They would even run roughshod through the Miami Heat in the NBA Finals. Had Durant and company faced a different incarnation of the Spurs, they would have beaten them and would have probably won the title that season.

Injury Season

As the offseason unfolded, Durant surprised everyone by backing out of the 2014 FIBA Basketball World Cup, citing that he needed some time to rest and prepare for the upcoming NBA season. By then, Durant had played the most minutes of any NBA player in the last five seasons. With the wear and tear slowly creeping up on him, Durant certainly needed to rest – he just received more than he had initially expected.

On October 11, 2014, Durant was diagnosed with a fractured foot that cost him the season's first 17 games, making his season debut on December 2, 2014, in a 112-104 loss to the New Orleans Pelicans. Durant made nine of his 18 shots from the field and three for eight from long distance to total 27 points. A couple of games later, he scored 28 points in the Thunder's 96-94 road win in Detroit on December 7, 2014.

But even though Durant was injured, the Thunder would nevertheless have to watch what Russell Westbrook could do as a lone leader as Kevin Durant was recuperating. However, even

Russ would have to sit out a few games as he was also hobbling from the injuries he had suffered two years before in the playoff series against the Rockets.

With both Kevin Durant and Russell Westbrook missing major time throughout the season, the OKC Thunder struggled during the early parts. They had to do well with what they had. Backup point guard Reggie Jackson was leading the charge in the absence of the duo. However, when Westbrook returned in February, he put on a show just the same as what Durant did a year ago.

In one of the best seasons for an NBA point guard, Westbrook was piling up statistics from all over the floor. He was racking up triple-doubles in bunches while also leading the NBA in scoring in the absence of his four-time scoring champion teammate. Proving true the words of Kevin Durant in his MVP speech, Westbrook was indeed MVP-caliber that season while KD was trying to recover.

Despite the fact that he was injured through most of the season, Durant still put up good numbers in the 27 games that he played. He averaged 25.4 points, 6.6 rebounds, and 4.1 assists. However, he could not shake off the lingering pains in his foot and was eventually shut down for the rest of the season in February.

Without Durant, the Oklahoma City Thunder would miss the playoffs for the first time since 2010. Not even Westbrook's monstrous season was able to make up for the loss of the 2014 NBA MVP.

In an April 2015 story by Sports Illustrated, Durant stated that it was the toughest year he ever had in his basketball career, telling reporters the following:

"Every day I tell myself we're going to look back on this and smile and laugh at it and recognize this is just an obstacle we had to climb over to get to where we want to get to. But I know for sure I'll be back. I know I'll put the work in. I know I'm never going to just quit on anything, so I'm going to keep working until I get back right."

Return to Form, Meltdown in the Conference Finals, Final Season in OKC

Similar to how critics questioned whether Russell Westbrook would be able to get back to full form after he was injured more than two seasons before, there were also growing concerns about whether Kevin Durant would be able to return to the MVP state he was at in 2014. There was no questioning his place as one of the top players and best scorers in the NBA. Nevertheless, his health was still a big concern as a similar tall and long superstar in the form of Yao Ming also suffered the same injury and would never be truly healthy again.

Another concern raised was how Durant and company would react to a new head coach in Billy Donovan, who replaced Scott Brooks after the latter was unable to lead the Thunder to a playoff berth in 2015. Though Donovan was new to the NBA, he was a legend in the college ranks in Florida and was famous for instilling a passing and ball-sharing mentality, which was far from the isolation-heavy strategies that Brooks had employed.

Finally, the question of who would be the alpha male for the Thunder was also a legitimate issue. There was no denying that Durant was the best player in the world in 2014 when he carried the Thunder all the way to the second-best record in the NBA, even without Westbrook for the majority of the season. But with Russ experiencing the same kind of scenario in 2015 sans the playoff appearance, both superstars were able to show that they could put up monstrous numbers and carry a team on their backs individually. With the two alpha superstars having been able to experience being the top guy in the Thunder, would Kevin Durant and Russell

Westbrook coexist under a new system? Or would Westbrook take the reins from Durant, who was still going to be sluggish due to the injury he had just recovered from?

Proving that he was a durable hard worker, Kevin Durant was able to join the lineup in time for the opening of the 2015-16 season. In the Thunder's second game, which was a double overtime win over the young Orlando Magic, Durant scored 43 points on 15 out of 30 shooting while collecting 12 rebounds. Meanwhile, Westbrook had 48 as the two superstars scored 40 apiece for the third time as a duo. As early as that game, there was no questioning the matured dynamic between KD and Russ. And there was also no doubt that Durant and Westbrook were the best duo the NBA had seen that era.

As Durant was steadily adjusting to the new team dynamics, he was also getting back to a similar form to when he won the MVP. Maintaining the same kind of consistency and efficiency he has always had in scoring, Durant would also improve his rebounding and would pass the ball at the same rate he did back in 2014 because Donovan's system employed a lot of sharing.

On December 10, 2015, Durant would have his first triple-double that season and his seventh overall. He had 25 points, 12 rebounds, and ten assists in that win against the Atlanta Hawks. Though his scoring would drop in December, Kevin Durant was playing in the system as he only shot what he could make while making sure he involved his teammates in the scoring parade. The scoring dip could be attributed to the sluggishness he was feeling after previously missing six games due to a hamstring injury. Though he was not the strongest scorer in December, he was named a co-winner of the Player of the Month award together with Westbrook.

One of Kevin Durant's better performances during the regular season came in front of the New York crowd on January 26, 2016. He would torch the Knicks for 44 points in an overtime victory while also grabbing 14 boards in that game. He would then end January by recording 33 points and 12 rebounds before being named Player of the Month again. Though it came in a loss against the top team in the NBA, Durant had 40 points and 15 rebounds against the Golden State Warriors and

Stephen Curry in a matchup between the two best players in the West.

Durant would be named a starter once again in the All-Star Game. He was starting together with Russell Westbrook. After scoring 23 in that game, Durant held on to his leadership regarding the most points scored on average in the All-Star Game. While he is still far from the overall leadership in points scored in the midseason classic, Durant's consistent performance while playing with his fellow All-Stars could only mean that he would soon find himself as the top overall scorer of the NBA All-Star Game.

As Kevin Durant continued his legendary consistency and efficiency in scoring, he would soon tie his idol Kobe Bryant for the most consecutive games of scoring at least 20 points. He did that on April 9 after scoring 31 points and grabbing ten rebounds against the Kings in a win. And by scoring 34 in his final game of the season, which was against the Lakers and the soon-to-retire Kobe Bryant, Durant broke his idol's mark with 64 straight games with at least 20 points.

While nobody could discount Durant's ability to put up at least 20 points per game, it was his overall improvement in all aspects of the game that made him a better player that season. With an improved dynamic partnership with Westbrook, Durant would even play the facilitator at times to give way to his superstar running mate. And as a testament to his matured rebounding skills, he was the Thunder's leading rebounder and even had seven straight games of double-digit rebounding.

Kevin Durant would average 28.2 points, a career high 8.2 rebounds, and 5.0 assists that season. And by shooting 50.5% from the floor, 38.7% from the three-point area, and 89.8% from the foul line, Durant would barely miss what could have been another 50-40-90 season for the efficient Thunder scorer. He would lead the OKC Thunder to a record of 55-27, which was good for the third seed in the West that saw historic seasons from both the Golden State Warriors (73-9) and the San Antonio Spurs (67-15).

Kevin Durant would open the postseason by leading the Thunder to a 38-point dominating win over the Dallas Mavericks. He scored 23 points in that game while only playing 26 minutes. Though the Thunder would drop

Game 2, Durant's 34 points in Game 3 got OKC back on track before beating the Mavs decisively two more times to win the series easily in five games. Despite a 15-13 record in their final 28 games after the All-Star break, the Thunder were peaking at the right moment after that series win over the Mavs.

Kevin Durant and his Thunder would be brought back down to earth and humbled by the mighty San Antonio Spurs in Game 1 of their second-round meeting. Losing by 32 points, Durant would only score 16 points in what was his worst performance all season long. Not to pull himself down even further, KD would have 28 points, seven rebounds, and four assists in a win over the Spurs in Game 2, albeit a controversial ending. San Antonio would get the series lead back by winning Game 3 in a close bout.

Not wanting to fall to a 1-3 deficit, Kevin Durant took it upon himself to lead his team back to force a competitive series against the Spurs. He would score 41 big points on 14 out of 25 shooting from the floor to beat San Antonio by 14 points and to tie the series 2-2. In Game 5, it was Westbrook's turn to put the team on his back by putting up 35 points, 11 rebounds, and nine assists to give OKC the series lead.

With the stars aligned for Kevin Durant and with all the chances of putting away the heavily favored San Antonio Spurs in Game 6 right on the home floor of the OKC Thunder, the four-time scoring champion would team together with Russell Westbrook to end the hopes of a soon-to-retire Tim Duncan of winning a sixth NBA title. Durant would score 37 points while Russ had 28 points and 12 assists for a Thunder team that had all the momentum and confidence in the world to finally win a title.

The road to the NBA Finals would only get tougher as the Oklahoma City Thunder would face the historic 73-9 Golden State Warriors in the Western Conference Finals. However, the Thunder were the favorites coming into that series. OKC had bigger players and a more athletic backcourt. Meanwhile, the Warriors heavily favored small ball while living and dying from the three-point line. Furthermore, the Warriors were not as healthy as the Thunder coming into that series.

The advantages of the Oklahoma City Thunder only became more evident as they drew first blood in the series. Durant would score 26 points, and it was Westbrook that took advantage of the weaker backcourt defense of the Warriors to record 27 points, 12 assists, and seven steals. Golden State would nevertheless win Game 2 by a significant margin.

In Game 3, the Thunder would run the Warriors to the ground by fully utilizing their athleticism and size to beat the title favorites by 28 points. Both Durant and Westbrook scored at least 30 in that game. KD, as efficient as ever, had 33 points on 10 out of 15 shooting from the field. He made all 12 of his free-throw attempts in that game. Using the same style that frustrated the Warriors, Oklahoma City would run to a 3-1 series lead after winning Game 4 decisively. However, that was the start of one of the worst meltdowns in playoff history.

Despite the 40 points and 31 markers from Kevin Durant and Russell Westbrook respectively, the OKC Thunder were not able to hold off a desperate Golden State Warriors from trying to get back to the series. Despite that loss, the Thunder still had two more games to close the series in their favor and to make the Finals for the second time since relocating to Oklahoma City.

Despite another good scoring effort from Durant in Game 6, the four-time league leading scorer struggled to shoot 32% from the floor as the Thunder was unable to stop Curry and Thompson from draining three-pointer after three-pointer to force a deciding Game 7 in Oakland. With the series tied at 3-3, the odds were not in favor of the OKC Thunder.

With the Thunder faltering in the second half and unable to defend the two-time winner and unanimous MVP Steph Curry, Oklahoma City would fall in Game 7 at the hands of the defending champions. In that closeout loss, Durant would score 27 points on only 19 shots as he spoiled his best chance of once again making it to the Finals. That loss to the Golden State Warriors sparked a chain of events that would lead to a significant power shift in the West and to a rebuilding process in Oklahoma City.

Kevin Durant was a free agent entering the 2016 offseason. Since he was one of the most elite players in the league at that time, Durant was the hottest commodity available in the market. He would have several suitors like the Boston Celtics, his hometown team of the Washington Wizards, the historic and famous team of the Los Angeles Lakers, and perennial contenders the San Antonio Spurs and the Golden State Warriors, who were the final two teams he had played against in the playoffs.

On their part, the OKC Thunder would sell a franchise legacy to Kevin Durant. He had the chance to become the historic face of the franchise until the day he retired. He may have even had the opportunity to win a title in Oklahoma City since the team would have still been intact for the following seasons had he intended to stay. Meanwhile, Kevin Durant had the chance to cause a major power surge if he decided to sign with either the Warriors or the Spurs. Both teams were already mightier than ever even without Durant. But signing the four-time scoring champion would only make either of those teams even better than they already were.

In the end, Kevin Durant would decide to sign with the Golden State Warriors, who promised to build a dynasty with him as one of the centerpieces. Despite losing to the Cavs in the Finals, the Warriors were still title favorites, even without KD in their lineup. Adding Durant only made them arguably the most dangerous team to have ever been assembled in league history as the superstar forward joined two-time MVP Stephen Curry and All-Stars Klay Thompson and Draymond Green to form a super team in Oakland.

But the decision of leaving Oklahoma City to join a great team for a chance to win a title was not a well-received one for Kevin Durant. Previously seen as the anti-LeBron James, Durant suddenly followed his rival's footsteps of joining a different team to suddenly form a championship contender just for an easy chance at a title.

The decision also led people to speculate whether Durant would have a good relationship with Russell Westbrook and whether the latter was his reason for leaving the Thunder. Nevertheless, KD would dispel any rumors about his bad relationship with Russ, saying that moving over to the Bay Area was strictly a basketball decision.

With Kevin Durant leaving the Thunder to join the Warriors, he blew his chance at becoming the historic face of the franchise, but nevertheless, improved his chances at solidifying his legacy as a winner in the NBA. Kevin Durant, hate him or love him, would be one of the most exciting and scrutinized figures in the 2016-17 season, especially now that he plays for the Warriors.

Chapter 5: International Play

Some of the greatest legends in the NBA have represented their home country during international play. The best example was the 1992 United States Dream Team which featured Larry Bird, Magic Johnson, Clyde Drexler, and Michael "Air" Jordan to help the US take the gold medal during the 1992 Summer Olympics in Barcelona, Spain.

There were some problems with the 2004 US Men's Olympic basketball team that only took the bronze medal, despite a roster that featured LeBron James, Tim Duncan, Carmelo Anthony, Amar'e Stoudemire, and Allen Iverson. Changes were made from the coaching staff, which included Larry Brown at the head with Gregg Popovich, Roy Williams, and Oliver Purnell as assistants.

While the 2008 squad won the gold medal in Beijing, China, head coach Mike Krzyzewski would establish a dominant group representing Team USA with a similar style that led him to become one of college basketball's greatest coaches. His current totals are 945 wins against 251 losses with the Duke Blue Devils and eight NCAA National Championships.

Fast forward to nearly a decade later. Durant would join his own "Dream Team" when he would don the red, white, and blue for the International Basketball Federation's (FIBA) 2010 Championships in Turkey. Even though this was considered the "B Team" compared to the US team that played in the 2008 Olympics, the 21-year-old Durant was the main attraction for the team that featured his Oklahoma City Thunder teammate Russell Westbrook, Chicago's Derrick Rose, Minnesota's Kevin Love, and LA Lakers' Lamar Odom.

In the preliminary round, the US swept everyone else in Group B for a 5-0 record. Durant was the leading scorer for the US in back-to-back games with 22 points in the team's 99-77 victory over Slovenia on August 29, 2010, and then scored another 27 points in the team's 70-68 win over Brazil the next day, in which Durant had a double-double with ten rebounds thrown in.

The US would move on and defeat Angola, 121-66, on September 16, 2010, in Round 16 to advance to the quarterfinals. While Chauncey Billups was the leading scorer with 19 points, Durant had 17 points of his own with five rebounds in only 19 minutes. Rudy Gay and Eric Gordon each had 17 points and just about everyone on the sideline scored some points against Angola.

Durant then became the leading star of the entire tournament with three straight quality games as the top-scoring player in each – starting with 33 points to help the United States defeat Russia 89-79 on September 9, 2010. In true Durant fashion, he made about 72 percent in the two-point region of the floor and another three for eight from beyond the arc. He also collected five defensive rebounds, two steals, and two blocked shots.

Durant followed that up with 38 points in 38 minutes on the court for the United States' 89-74 win over Lithuania on September 11, 2010, during the semifinal round. He made 14 out of 25 from the field with nine rebounds. The next day, the USA was able to capture the FIBA gold medal after defeating the home nation, Turkey, 81-64 on September 12, 2010. Durant led the team with 28 points, five rebounds, and two blocks. He also shot 58.8 percent from the field, most of which came from long-distance as he shot 7 out of 13 from behind the three-point line.

Durant was brought back with a lot of the NBA's best players to make it more like an All-Star team for the 2012 Summer Olympics. LeBron James, Kobe Bryant, and Carmelo Anthony were on the squad, along with Durant's Thunder teammates Russell Westbrook and James Harden.

Before the Olympics in Spain, the US played a series of exhibition games starting with a 113-59 blowout of the Dominic

Republic on July 12, 2012, in Paradise, Nevada, in which Durant had a double-double with 24 points and ten rebounds. Durant was also the leading scorer for the US in a 118-78 win over Argentina (27 points) July 22, 2012, in Spain.

The US then entered the preliminary round in Group A going undefeated, starting with a 98-71 victory over France on July 29, 2012, wherein Durant led the game with 22 points. Durant was also the leading scorer with 28 points as the United States defeated Argentina 126-97 on August 6, 2012.

In the semifinals, Durant was the leader for the US in a 109-83 win over Argentina on August 10, 2012. Durant was one of five players to score in double figures for the game – James, 18; Anthony, 18; Bryant, 13, and Chris Paul, 10.

Durant shined the best to help the US defeat the home country, Spain, 107-100 on August 12, 2012 – leading all players with 30 points and nine rebounds. Half of his points came from behind the three-point line with five deep baskets and shooting 9 for ten free throws.

Overall, the US was undefeated (8-0) with an average of 116 points and an average margin of 32.1 points, which was just the fifth highest in Olympic history for Team USA. While stars like James, Bryant, and Anthony were building on their already existing international basketball legacies by repeating their gold medal in the 2008 Olympics, Durant was a key contributor and is likely a top choice to come back to Team USA for the 2016 Summer Olympics in Rio de Janeiro, Brazil.

Durant was invited to play for Team USA to defend the country's gold medal in the 2014 FIBA Championships in Spain, but Durant pulled out claiming mental and physical exhaustion after the NBA Western Conference Finals loss to the San Antonio Spurs after an 81-game season. It was an understandable decision for Durant to choose to rest.

The United States lost some star power as compared to the 2012 Olympics, or to the 2010 FIBA Championships, although there were some key contributors with Stephan Curry, Klay Thompson, Kyrie Irving, and DeMarcus Cousins. The US was still able to clinch the gold medal after defeating Serbia 129-92, once again going undefeated through pool play and the rest of the tournament.

Chapter 6: Durant's Personal Life

Kevin Durant is still single, though he was previously engaged to the WNBA's Minnesota Lynx player Monica Wright in 2013. Both were highly-touted prep basketball stars from the Washington DC area, but because their counties are about an hour's drive apart, their paths did not cross until the 2006 McDonald's All-American All-Stars in San Diego wherein they both participated. What began as friendship ended up in a relationship that led to a wedding engagement between the two basketball stars.

However, the couple separated almost one year after the engagement because of what Wright said was Durant's inability to "sacrifice" his lifestyle for her. Other sources cited religious beliefs as the reason, while there were also those who claimed that Kevin Durant was unfaithful to Wright during their engagement. After the break-up, Wright claimed to have received a lot of criticism, but said that her faith in God helped her overcome them and move on with her life.

Aside from big brother Tony, Durant has two other siblings: his brother, Rayvonne, and sister, Brianna. It is Tony that Kevin is closest to, not only because they grew up together, but because they shared the same passion: basketball.

Like Kevin, Tony Durant was a basketball player, but the two never played together on the same team because Tony was three years older than Kevin. When Tony finished his freshman season at Suitland High School in Forestville, Maryland, he wanted to go out on his own, so he transferred to St. John's Military School in Salina, Kansas. Tony moved on to play for Butler Community College, and then for two seasons at Towson.

After Kevin had signed his first NBA contract, he bought his brother, Tony, a brand new black 2007 Dodge Charger. According to Kevin, the vehicle was in payment of a debt which he owed his brother when they were just kids. That debt emanated from a broken glass light switch door in their living room which Kevin caused after throwing a boot at Tony during a brotherly fight. Kevin needed $10 to repair the damage, but because he did not have any money at that time, he borrowed money from Tony, who was then working part-time at McDonald's. Ten years later, Tony's $10 became a brand new Dodge Charger.

Immediately after signing his rookie NBA contract with the Oklahoma City Thunder, Kevin Durant signed a $60 million shoe endorsement deal with Nike, which was the second largest rookie shoe contract since LeBron James' $90M. Before Durant signed that deal, Adidas had a bigger offer of $70 million. Nevertheless, Durant chose Nike because he had personally worn Nike basketball shoes ever since he was a kid.

Durant grew up in the Washington area, but surprisingly, his favorite team as a kid was the Toronto Raptors because he was such a huge fan of former Toronto Raptors' franchise player Vince Carter. When Durant was a child, Carter was throwing down one spectacular dunk after another, earning him the nickname "Vinsanity." Durant admired how Carter brought the Raptors from a franchise team to a team that almost made the finals.

While he has no visible tattoos when he wears his basketball uniform, Kevin Durant's back, chest, and stomach are covered with ink. Durant is the owner of a massive tattoo on his back. That ink work features an angel holding a basketball, an image of Jesus Christ, and a Bible verse. On his left chest is a tattoo of his mother's name, Wanda, with a rose above it, while opposite it is the name of his grandmother, Barbara, which has a dove above it.

Kevin Durant's jersey number 35 was retired by the University of Texas shortly after he was drafted by the Seattle SuperSonics. Durant wore number 35 when he was with the Sonics; he still wears the same number now that he is with the OKC Thunder. The reason why Kevin Durant wears the jersey number 35 is to honor his earliest coach and childhood mentor Charles "Chucky" Craig who was shot to death when Durant was still in high school. Chucky was always a peacemaker in the neighborhood. So when one of his friends got involved in a scuffle on April 30, 2005, he broke up the fight. However, his friend's enemy came back to the neighborhood later that day driving a car. When he recognized Chucky from the scuffle, he pulled out a gun and shot Chucky Craig multiple times in the back, causing his immediate death.

When Kevin asked his godfather Taras Brown about the best way he could pay tribute to Chucky on the basketball court, they both agreed that Kevin would ditch his number 24 jersey (which was the number Chucky initially gave him when he was nine years old in the Recreation Center) in favor of the number 35. Chucky was 35 years old when he was shot dead on that fateful day in 2005. Durant said that Chucky's death made him furious, and he poured out that anger on the basketball court against his opponents. In a way, because Chucky's death brought out the fire in Durant, it accelerated his ascent to the NBA. Durant has worn jersey number 35 ever since his college days at Texas. One week after being drafted by the Seattle SuperSonics, the

University of Texas retired jersey number 35 in honor of their freshman sensation, Kevin Durant.

When Chucky was still alive, Kevin Durant told him and his godfather, Taras Brown, that he wanted both of them to be with him in the green room on NBA draft day. Unfortunately, Chucky was not there when the Thunder drafted Durant second overall in 2007. Nevertheless, with the number 35 pasted to his back every single game, Durant keeps Chucky alive each time he steps onto a basketball court.

Chapter 7: Impact on Basketball

Durant's clean image has made him one of the NBA's top salesmen. In 2013, sales for Kevin Durant's signature Nike shoes soared 400% from $35M to $175M according to Forbes.com. Although those figures still paled in comparison to LeBron's total of $300M shoe sales last year, there is no doubt that Durant is coming into his own as an endorser while he is coming into his own as an NBA superstar. Furthermore, since Durant was named 2014 NBA MVP, those numbers are expected to rise further at the end of 2016.

His value as an endorser came to its peak earlier this year when new shoe player, Under Armour, offered him a ridiculous $300M shoe deal as his seven-year contract with Nike was expiring. However, Nike simply could not let Durant walk away to Under Armour, so they matched the offer with a deal that is reportedly around the same figure as Under Armour. This makes Durant the highest-paid shoe endorser on the planet.

Recently, Kevin Durant added fast food drive-in chain Sonic to his long list of endorsements. Since transferring to Jay-Z's Roc Nation promotions, Durant has become an endorser for Orange Leaf, the zero calorie sparkling water brand Sparkling Ice, and Kind Healthy snack bars. Durant's other prior existing endorsements include Skullcandy headphones, the NBA 2K video game, BBVA Compass Bank, Panini, The Oklahoma Department of Health, and an underwear collection called Neff. Last year, Durant made an estimated $14M in endorsements. That amount is expected to balloon when the figures for 2016 are released.

Durant's endorsement star is clearly on the rise, especially after winning the 2014 MVP. But it is not just because of his basketball success; it is because he has never forgotten to give back.

In 2012, Durant launched the Kevin Durant Charity Foundation to help financially burdened kids and their families. The focus of the foundation is to help kids stay off the streets by engaging them in neighborhood activities. The foundation has three branches: one for single mothers, another for education, and the last one is called "Kevin's Christmas." Just this March, Kind Healthy Snacks donated $1M to the Kevin Durant Charity Foundation to create specialized education and after-school programs that would teach participating youth to be "strong and kind."

Durant's kind and big heart was displayed in 2013 when Oklahoma City was ravaged by a tornado. That tornado ripped through Oklahoma City's suburban Moore and killed 24 people. However, just as the tornado blitzed the city, so did Durant's help. Eager to help the devastated area, he immediately donated $1M for tornado relief. That sparkling voluntary gesture moved the rest of the NBA community and more. The Thunder organization also donated $1M, and so did the NBA. Durant did not stop there. He reached out to Nike and the shoe company also gave its $1 million share.

The Moore Relief was not just one of the examples of Durant's philanthropy. It also showed the genuineness of his person and the impact of his popularity. There is no question about his impact on the game. Durant's unique combination of height and skill have revolutionized the power forward and small forward position. Durant's impact on the game is more than just as a player; it is also as a person. The image and reputation that he solidly built as a young kid in Maryland have carried over through the years without a doubt. He's proved to the world that a simple and humble kid can achieve greatness if he works hard and remains grounded despite all the success he has had.

Chapter 8: Kevin Durant's Legacy and Future

The NBA has found a new front man who is unlike his peers in Kevin Durant. While other NBA stars constantly look for the bigger market cities to get better pay and more exposure, Durant is one who looks like he will stay in low-key Oklahoma City for the rest of his career, and why not? Durant and Oklahoma City are a perfect match: quiet, low-key, humble, and hardworking.

Despite all the success that he has achieved in his basketball career, Kevin Durant's feet remain planted on the ground. He has remained humble despite all the accomplishments that he has made because he was brought up that way by his mother, Wanda, and grandmother, Barbara. Durant grew up in a closely-knit family, and he has retained the value of family and relationships. This is the reason Durant can be seen talking candidly to fans and reporters alike. He can be seen fist bumping with kids and high-fiving with fans before games. This is the reason why we see him hug and kiss his mother after basketball games.

Durant's humility was never more in the spotlight than in the 2014 playoffs when he was called Mr. Unreliable by an Oklahoma newspaper after the Thunder struggled in their playoff series against the Memphis Grizzlies. Instead of reacting violently to the media, Durant kept his composure and scored 36 points in the following game to send that series to a Game 7. The Thunder would win that series, but Durant clearly won the hearts of NBA fans who were witness to his supreme humility.

Durant's refusal to be a part of the egoistic basketball superstardom does stem from his early days as a basketball player. He was always the tallest in his class when he was a kid, but no school took a fancy to him or saw his potential. His mother, Wanda, says that her son had to work harder and harder to become a good basketball player. He was not discouraged in basketball, just like he was not with life. His single mother raised him and his brother on her own, and he saw how hard she worked to give them a future. It is that same hard work that brought Durant out of the Saint Pleasant Recreation Center to take the world by storm.

Durant always had this motto which his godfather Taras Brown instilled in him when he was a kid: Hard work beats talent when talent fails to work hard. Other than Kobe Bryant, there may be no other player in the history of the game who works on his game as hard, even if he is already great. Ever since he was a kid, Durant found his purpose on a basketball court. As the NBA's face for the years to come, he still continues to work hard on improving his game. Growing and working hard to improve never stops and neither will Kevin Durant.

Hard work and humility are the two core values that have endeared the public's perception of Durant. His unassuming attitude was what made him the anti-LeBron. Remember when James chose to leave small city Cleveland for South Beach? Durant decided to stay in OKC. Again, we go back to where we started: Rivalries.

LeBron James and Kevin Durant may not be as bitter rivals as Magic and Bird were in the 1980's, but their paths have crossed because of their quest for excellence. LeBron and his Heat beat Durant and the Thunder in Kevin's only NBA Finals appearance so far, so these on-court clashes have added to the storyline of their rivalry. When James won three of his four MVP awards, Durant finished second. Last season, Durant and James went neck and neck once again, but Durant finally proved that he could beat James, and winning the 2014 MVP battle was perhaps just the beginning.

The rivalry of Durant and James has defined the NBA in the last few years. While most pundits still consider LeBron as the Alpha and Durant as the Beta, the latter is slowly bridging that gap quietly and without much fanfare. It is scary to think about

Kevin Durant as a basketball player when he finally reaches the prime of his career.

The rivalry between the two players might have died down when Durant was injured in 2015 and when LeBron James formed his rivalry with Steph Curry of the Golden State Warriors. However, one would think that the rivalry would be revived since KD now suits up for the Warriors after signing with them in the offseason of 2016.

Though his decision to sign with the Warriors might have tarnished his reputation as the once popular and loved member of the Oklahoma City Thunder, Kevin Durant was, and is always, all about basketball and winning games. The end goal for him is to win a championship, and he found his best chances in Oakland. Though he might receive heavy scrutiny and criticism for his decision, Durant will undoubtedly still be one of the best scorers and players in basketball history.

Final Word/About the Author

I was born and raised in Norwalk, Connecticut. Growing up, I could often be found spending many nights watching basketball, soccer, and football matches with my father in the family living room. I love sports and everything that sports can embody. I believe that sports are one of most genuine forms of competition, heart, and determination. I write my works to learn more about influential athletes in the hopes that from my writing, you the reader can walk away inspired to put in an equal if not greater amount of hard work and perseverance to pursue your goals. If you enjoyed *Kevin Durant: The Inspiring Story of One of Basketball's Greatest Small Forwards,* please leave a review! Also, you can read more of my works on *Rob Gronkowski, Brett Favre, Calvin Johnson, Drew Brees, J.J. Watt, Colin Kaepernick, Aaron Rodgers, Peyton Manning, Tom Brady, Russell Wilson, Michael Jordan, LeBron James, Kyrie Irving, Klay Thompson, Stephen Curry, Russell Westbrook, Anthony Davis, Chris Paul, Blake Griffin, Kobe Bryant, Joakim Noah, Scottie Pippen, Carmelo Anthony, Kevin Love, Grant Hill, Tracy McGrady, Vince Carter, Patrick Ewing, Karl Malone, Tony Parker, Allen Iverson, Hakeem Olajuwon, Reggie Miller, Michael Carter-Williams, John Wall, James Harden, Tim Duncan, Steve Nash, Draymond Green, Kawhi Leonard,*

Dwyane Wade, Ray Allen, Pau Gasol, Dirk Nowitzki, Jimmy Butler, Paul Pierce, Manu Ginobili, Pete Maravich, Larry Bird, Kyle Lowry, Jason Kidd, David Robinson, LaMarcus Aldridge, Derrick Rose, Paul George, Kevin Garnett, Chris Paul and Marc Gasol in the Kindle Store. If you love basketball, check out my website at claytongeoffreys.com to join my exclusive list where I let you know about my latest books and give you lots of goodies.

Like what you read? Please leave a review!

I write because I love sharing the stories of influential people like Kevin Durant with fantastic readers like you. My readers inspire me to write more so please do not hesitate to let me know what you thought by leaving a review! If you love books on life, basketball, or productivity, check out my website at claytongeoffreys.com to join my exclusive list where I let you know about my latest books. Aside from being the first to hear about my latest releases, you can also download a free copy of *33 Life Lessons: Success Principles, Career Advice & Habits of Successful People.* See you there!

Clayton

References

[i] "Kevin Durant". *Draft Express.*

[ii] Joseph, Adi. "Kevin Durant Scouting Report". *NBAdraft.net.* Web

[iii] Young, Royce. "Remember the Time When KD Couldn't Bench 185? Yeah, He Can Now". *Daily Thunder.* 10 November 2010. Web

[iv] Brooks, Maurice. "Oden Stands Tall Among the Prospects". *NBA.com.* 2007. Web

[v] "Strength Training With Kevin Durant". *Stack.* 1 February 2009. Web

[vi] Lantz, Jessica. "Kevin Durant, Chris Paul and Friends Lift Lockout Blues in Oklahoma City Game". *SB Nation.* 24 October 2011. Web

[vii] Shoals, Bethlehem. "Kevin Durant is Winning the Lockout". *GQ.* 15 August 2011. Web

[viii] "NBA Superstars LeBron James and Kevin Durant Team Up for Workout". *Stack.* 10 November 2011. Web

[ix] Young, Royce. "Kevin Durant: I'm Tired of Being Second… I'm done with it". *CBS Sports.* 23 April 2013. Web

[x] Durant, Kevin. "Kevin Durant: The Oklahoma City Thunder Star's Complete MVP Speech". *The Oklahoman.* 13 May 2014. Web

Made in the USA
San Bernardino, CA
20 December 2017